Catholic

IN AN ECUMENICAL AND INTERRELIGIOUS SOCIETY

Evangelization

SECRETARIAT FOR EVANGELIZATION

United States Conference of Catholic Bishops

Washington, DC

The document *Catholic Evangelization in an Ecumenical and Interreligious Society* was developed as a resource by the Committee on Evangelization of the United States Conference of Catholic Bishops (USCCB). It was reviewed by the committee chairman, Bishop Edward J. Slattery, and has been authorized by the undersigned.

Msgr. William P. Fay
General Secretary
USCCB

Excerpts from *Moral Grandeur and Spiritual Audacity* by Abraham Joshua Heschel © 1996 by Sylvia Heschel. Reprinted by permission of Farrar, Straus and Giroux, LLC, New York.

Excerpts from *Truth and Community: Diversity and Its Limits in the Ecumenical Movement* by Michael Kinnamon © 1988, W. B. Eerdmans Publishing, Grand Rapids, Michigan, are used with permission of the publisher.

Excerpts from *Christianity and the Religions: From Confrontation to Dialogue* by Fr. Jacques Dupuis, SJ, trans. Phillip Berryman © 2002, Orbis Books, Maryknoll, New York, are used with permission of the publisher.

First Printing, June 2004

ISBN 1-57455-641-X

CONTENTS

INTRODUCTION

I n March 2003, the United States Conference of Catholic Bishops' Committee on Evangelization (hereafter BCEV) explored how it might address the complex and sensitive issue of Catholic evangelization in an ecumenical and interreligious society. Many Catholics are asking, "How can I invite non-Catholics to explore a relationship with Christ in the Catholic Church and fulfill my responsibility to be both ecumenical and respectful toward other faith communities?" Listening with a loving heart and learning from others is essential in any genuine relationship. This is the starting point for proclaiming the Gospel and for ecumenical and interreligious dialogue. Proclaiming the Gospel is not synonymous with, but rather essential to evangelization; and ecumenical and interreligious dialogue is another essential aspect of evangelization.

Since the Second Vatican Council, people of faith have made great strides in addressing this apparent dilemma. The Church's very identity is found in its mission to evangelize. As the United States Conference of Catholic Bishops (USCCB) statement *Go and Make Disciples: A National Plan and Strategy for Catholic Evangelization in the United States* (GMD) notes, "Knowing Christ Jesus and belonging to his Church are not the same as believing anything else and belonging to any other community."[1] Our message does not mean that others' faith and sincerity are not genuine, nor does this take away from the need for us to be clear about the truth of our message (no. 32). As Pope John Paul II reminds us, "It is necessary to keep these two truths together, namely, the real possibility of salvation in Christ for all humankind and the necessity of the Church for salvation. Both these truths help us to understand the one mystery of salvation."[2]

In the United States, our society today is blessed by a diversity of faiths and Christian traditions. This diversity affects our family life, our schools, our city traditions, and our workplaces. All faith traditions are being challenged by the ongoing secularization of our society and its impact on religious traditions and our very notions of faith and religion. Yet for us to respond to this complex issue in the pews of our own Church, we must open people's eyes to the possibilities of how God is calling each of us to respond as Catholics in fostering respect and greater understanding of people of faith who are not Catholic.

As Catholic Christians, we are forever indebted to our Jewish brothers and sisters, the first to hear the Word of God. They are the "Chosen

People, to whom the covenants and promises were made and who, in view of divine choice, are a people most dear to God" (GMD, no. 43).

With regard to people of other non-Christian religions, *Go and Make Disciples* states,

> People of other non-Christian religions also have the right to hear the Gospel, as missionaries have brought it over the centuries. God's plan of salvation also includes the Muslims who profess the faith of Abraham and, together with us, adore the one, merciful God. Then there are those who through no fault of their own do not know the Gospel of Christ or his Church but nevertheless seek God with sincere hearts and seek to do God's will as they know it. Interreligious dialogue presents an opportunity to learn about other religious traditions and to explain our own. Such dialogue, however, must never be a camouflage for proselytizing. Rather, it should be approached with utmost respect and sensitivity. (no. 44)

On the other hand, Catholics need ongoing catechesis in order to know enough about the Church, its teachings, and its traditions to contribute to a mutual understanding with others.

Since the mid-1960s, people of faith have been seeing more clearly that the Holy Spirit is at work through the ecumenical movement, "calling churches and ecclesial communities into ever-deeper communion through dialogues and cooperation. While recognizing that the life of other Christian communions can truly bring about a life of grace, we nevertheless cannot ignore all that still divides us" (GMD, no. 42).

At the beginning of this new millennium, we must acknowledge the complexity of our beliefs together as we approach the mystery of God that has been revealed to us and our responsibility to live out this mystery. Throughout his papacy, John Paul II has continued to encourage dialogue with all who are not Catholic. He demonstrates for all of us the sacredness of ecumenical and interreligious dialogue by praying publicly with and for people of faith who are not Catholic, and by visiting their houses of prayer and worship.

Within the Catholic Church in the United States, this complex issue of diversity is becoming an ordinary way of life. The demographics for all faith traditions are changing, and in this environment, these faith traditions run the risk of losing their identity. From our own experience as Catholics, we have seen mixed-faith marriages continue to increase. We see a new complexity in Catholic life as people of other faiths unite with Catholics in the intimate life of marriage. Our Catholic schools are changing from a time when most students in them were Catholics, to the present reality, in which over 50 percent of the students are non-Catholic in some areas. Our Catholic Charities and Catholic Campaign for Human Development continue to foster great respect and cooperation among people of all faiths. The sick who come to Catholic hospitals experience a warm welcome and the spirit of genuine Christian hospitality in an environment that provides the best of health care. These are a few areas where the fabric of Catholic life and mission is significantly impacted by the diversity of our ecumenical and interreligious society.

In March 2003, the BCEV began considering this complex issue of Catholic evangelization in an ecumenical and interreligious society. Fr. Arthur Kennedy, the executive director of the USCCB Secretariat for Ecumenical and Interreligious Affairs, met with the BCEV and provided us with excellent advice and resources for addressing this issue. The committee decided to address this theme with a convocation for diocesan evangelization directors, held in February 2003 in Louisville, Kentucky. Fr. Kennedy and Fr. John Hurley, the executive director of the USCCB Secretariat for Evangelization, collaborated on this project. Through their collaboration and the focus of the convocation, diocesan ecumenical directors also were invited to attend. Although the convocation would be limited to the two groups noted above, the BCEV intended to provide the presentations as a resource to a much wider audience.

In this document, you will find the beginnings of our attempt to continue to foster a greater understanding and respect for people of faith who are not Catholic and, at the same time, to show how such understanding and respect have implications for any genuine Catholic evangelization.

The convocation's organizers welcomed as keynote speaker Bishop Stephen Blaire of the Diocese of Stockton, California, who serves as the chairman of the USCCB Committee on Ecumenical and Interreligious Affairs. In addition to Bishop Blaire's keynote address on "Catholic Evangelization in an Ecumenical and Interreligious Society," three other major addresses were given: "Ecumenical Implications for Catholic Evangelization," "Jewish Relations and Catholic Evangelization," and "Interreligious Implications for Catholic Evangelization." We welcome this opportunity to present readers with these four unique contributions to the effort to foster ongoing respect for and understanding of the beliefs of non-Catholics, an effort without which we cannot be true to the essential mission of the Church in our society today.

In addition to the aforementioned four presentations, this collection includes a homily by the Rev. Keith Marsh, rector of Christ Church Episcopal Cathedral in Louisville, Kentucky. This was delivered at an ecumenical prayer service, as part of the convocation at the Cathedral of the Assumption, where Archbishop Thomas Kelly presided.

I would like to express my gratitude on behalf of all those who gathered for this convocation. Our thanks go to our host, Archbishop Thomas Kelly, and his directors in the Archdiocese of Louisvillee offices of Ecumenical and Interreligious Relations, Multicultural Ministry, and Worship. Their support and assistance were critical to the success of the convocation.

The BCEV hopes that these presentations will assist Catholics in bringing about a greater understanding of the Catholic Church's essential mission of being a resource for those involved in the Church's ministry, which touches the lives of people of other faiths and other Christian communions. This tool will help directors of evangelization and ecumenical and interreligious ministries; directors for the Rite of Christian Initiation of Adults, hospital ministry, and marriage preparation; principals in our Catholic schools; and all our Church's social programs, to name a few.

Let us pray that the Holy Spirit will continue to guide us in preaching the Gospel with the utmost respect and understanding, as we approach all men and women.

Most Rev. Edward J. Slattery
Bishop of Tulsa
Chairman, USCCB Committee on Evangelization

NOTES

1 United States Conference of Catholic Bishops, *Go and Make Disciples: A National Plan and Strategy for Catholic Evangelization in the United States.* Tenth Anniversary Spanish and English Edition (Washington, DC: USCCB, 2002), no. 32. Subsequent citations are given in the text.

2 John Paul II, *On the Permanent Validity of the Church's Missionary Mandate (Redemptoris Missio)* (Washington, DC: Libreria Editrice Vaticana–USCCB, 1998), no. 9.

KEYNOTE PRESENTATION

CATHOLIC EVANGELIZATION IN AN ECUMENICAL AND INTERRELIGIOUS SOCIETY

BISHOP STEPHEN J. BLAIRE

I want to thank the United States Conference of Catholic Bishops' Committee on Evangelization for the kind invitation to offer some reflections on Catholic evangelization in an ecumenical and inter-religious society. Please keep in mind that my position as chair of the Bishops' Committee for Ecumenical and Interreligious Affairs is only a little over a year long, so my experience is limited. However, I have been well served by a highly competent staff.

Let me begin by setting the stage with two important scenarios that are taking place in the United States in which the Catholic Church is an important actor.

This past month, a major organizational meeting was held at Camp Allen outside of Houston, Texas. Fifty participants representing over thirty Christian churches attended the meeting. Ten of those present were Roman Catholic. The purpose of the gathering was to move forward with the establishment of the document *Christian Churches Together in the U.S.A.* The goal was to create not another bureaucratic structure with all kinds of offices and staff, but rather, to create a forum for participation in which each member would be able to find a home. The organization would be constituted by its participants and serve as a forum for them.

In other words, it would not be the creation of some kind of new mega-church organization. It would be a participatory alliance. Each participant would be part of a faith family designation that would allow broad-based representation without ecclesiological definition. The five families would be Evangelical/Pentecostal, Historic Protestant, Historic Racial/Ethnic, Orthodox, and Roman Catholic. As you can see, we Catholics would be our own family.

To be a member church or Christian community or Christian organization would require (1) belief in the Lord Jesus Christ as God and Savior according to the Scriptures; (2) worship and service of the one God, Father, Son, and Holy Spirit; and (3) desire to seek ways to work together in order to present a more credible Christian witness in and to the world.

Without going into further detail, I would say that the organizing document is in accord with our Catholic understanding of evangelization. *Christian Churches Together* has as its purpose to enable churches to grow closer together in Christ in order to strengthen Christian witness in the world. As soon as twenty-five churches or Christian communities join, the organization will come into being. It is anticipated that this should happen within the next year and a half. I presented the proposal to the bishops of the United States this past November and hope that we will have a decision from the conference of bishops in the not-too-distant future.

The second important happening will take place in San Francisco in March. The bishops' Subcommittee on Interreligious Dialogue will sponsor the second Institute for Bishops on Islam and Catholic-Muslim Relations. The institute will offer bishops the opportunity to study the Qumran and documents of the Catholic Church on relations with Muslims and to reflect on contemporary issues. We cannot underestimate the importance of this type of meeting. There seems to be little doubt that, as we move through this century, the two major religions of the world—Christianity and Islam—will grow at an enormous pace.

It is self-evident that the Catholic Church lives in an ecumenical and interreligious world and will continue to do so in an ever-expansive way.

I suspect that the theme of our gathering this week has been suggested by some down-to-earth questions like these: Do I try to persuade my Methodist neighbor to join the Catholic Church? Is it okay for our youth to go to a Baptist Youth Fellowship? Do I try to bring back to the Catholic Church the baptized (but not catechized) Hispanic who has joined an Evangelical ecclesial community? Do I seek to convert my Muslim co-worker? Can Jews be saved? Do the Passion narratives in the Gospels give rise to antisemitism?

Will I answer these questions directly? Not now. What I hope to do is to offer a few clarifying thoughts from a Catholic perspective on ecumenism and interreligious relationships vis-à-vis evangelization. Hopefully this will provide some light on how to approach these questions.

I undertake this task with hesitation, because we are talking about the living experience and identity of the Catholic Church in a world of over a billion Christians, a billion members of Islam, and millions of other adherents to various religious traditions—let alone Christianity—in a highly secularized, western part of the world.

Very simply, evangelization is the mission of the Church. Ecumenism is a movement within the Church; interreligious affairs involve relationships of dialogue and cooperation. Ultimately, we are dealing with the matter of salvation. God is the Savior of the world through his Son Jesus Christ, who died for all. How does this play out in terms of ecumenism and interreligious relations? One must approach this topic with great humility, guided by the teachings of the Second Vatican Council, and with profound awareness that we are talking about a work of the Holy Spirit.

In reflecting on Catholic evangelization, I always go back to Pope Paul VI's great apostolic exhortation *On Evangelization in the Modern World* (*Evangelii Nuntiandi*) (EN).[1] In it, the pope reminds us clearly that evangelization is the essential mission of the Church. It is the grace and vocation proper to the Church, her deepest identity. So rich, complex, and dynamic is the reality of evangelization that one cannot restrict its definition in any way.

Paul VI wrote that the elements of proclaiming Christ to those who do not know him, of preaching, of catechesis, and of conferring Baptism and the other sacraments are so important that they sometimes are identified with evangelization. But for the Church, he said, "evangelizing means bringing the Good News into all the strata of humanity, and through its influence transforming humanity from within and making it new" (EN, no. 18). Evangelization is so all-encompassing and complex as to include "the renewal of humanity, witness, explicit proclamation, inner adherence, entry into the community, acceptance of signs, apostolic initiative" (EN, no. 24).

If you couple what Paul VI said with what Pope John Paul II has said about the new evangelization, you realize the great challenge to accomplish this mission of the Church in new ways, in new times, and, I might add, in a multiplicity of ways.

In particular, John Paul II has linked the future of the new evangelization closely to ecumenism. In these twilight years of the pope's life, numerous themes have been identified as significant to his Petrine ministry. Right at the top has been his dedication to the ecumenical endeavor that all be one in Christ. In *The Church in Europe* (*Ecclesia in Europa*), he wrote, "Therefore I once again make my own the words written by Paul VI to Ecumenical Patriarch Athenagoras I: 'May the Holy Spirit guide us along the way of reconciliation, so that the unity of our Churches may become an ever more radiant sign of hope and consolation for all mankind.'"[2]

Likewise, John Paul II places great importance on interreligious dialogue. He is clear that such dialogue does not replace the proclamation of the Gospel and missionary activity ad gentes, but that this missionary duty does not keep us from listening with a profound willingness in dialogue. In the document *On the Permanent Validity of the Church's Missionary Mandate* (*Redemptoris Missio*), John Paul II acknowledges that "the boundaries between pastoral care of the faithful, new evangelization and specific missionary activity are not clearly definable, and it is unthinkable to create barriers between them or to put them into watertight compartments."[3]

Let me now say a few words about the nature of ecumenism, the import of interreligious dialogue, its place in the mission of the Church, and how it plays out in terms of evangelization.

In the early days of the Second Vatican Council, on December 1, 1962, a resolution was approved by the fathers of the Council to prepare one document on ecumenism rather than to have chapters in various other documents. The fathers in this way gave approval to the ecumenical purpose of the Council as had been proposed by Pope John XXIII. This did not mean that the "restoration of unity among all Christians" was the purpose of the Council, but one of the tasks of the Council was to promote this unity. The lack of unity among Christians

---

Interreligious dialogue presents an opportunity to learn about other religious traditions and to explain our own. Such dialogue, however, must never be a camouflage for proselytizing. Rather, it should be approached with utmost respect and sensitivity. Catholics earnestly share their faith in Jesus Christ, which gives meaning to their lives, praying for that good day, known to God alone, when all peoples will address the Lord in a single voice and serve God with one accord.

—*Go and Make Disciples: A National Plan and Strategy for Catholic Evangelization in the United States* (Washington, DC: USCCB, 2002), no. 43.

---

was seen as contradictory to the will of Christ. Jesus' prayer had been that all may be one so that the world would believe that he had been sent by the Father. The underlying ecclesiology was that of *communio*, in which the Holy Spirit is the principle of unity joining the faithful together with each other in Christ. There is only one Church of Christ, and as the *Dogmatic Constitution on the Church* (*Lumen Gentium*) says, it subsists in the Catholic Church. But elements of the one Church are also present outside the Catholic Church, in other churches or ecclesial communities.[4]

Since the Second Vatican Council, the understanding of the Church as *communio*, the articulation of the mission of the Church as evangelization, and the ecumenical movement have all been dynamic components interacting to carry out the will of Christ as expressed in the seventeenth chapter of John's Gospel. Listen to this paragraph from *That They May Be One* (*Ut Unum Sint*), in which the Holy Father quotes from the Congregation of the Doctrine of the Faith's *Letter to the Bishops of the Catholic Church on Some Aspects of the Church Understood as Communion*:

> the Church is not a reality closed in on herself. Rather, she is permanently open to missionary and ecumenical endeavor, for she is sent to the world to announce and witness, to make present and spread the mystery of communion which is essential to her, and to gather all people and all things into Christ, so as to be for all an "inseparable sacrament of unity."[5]

Can we not conclude that the purpose of ecumenism and evangelization are the same: that all be one in Christ? Since evangelization embraces all that the Church does, and all the Church's activity must be in accord with her mission, would it not also be correct to say that the ecumenical endeavor is an activity integral to fulfilling the Church's mission in and to the world? The Council documents, Paul VI, and John Paul II all have emphasized that a people divided are an impediment to evangelization, and that if we are going to proclaim the Gospel to the world, we must be committed to working for reconciliation between Christians.

Let us move on now to some reflections about interreligious dialogue. This is a much more difficult subject to approach in terms of evangelization. It requires great sensitivity due to the complexity involved in relating to the religions of the world. We enter into dialogue with great respect and esteem but not forgetting, as Paul VI said, that these religions "have the right to know the riches of the mystery of Christ" (EN, no. 53).

We always keep central in our minds and hearts that Jesus Christ is the Savior of the world. But we can never set aside an overriding principle that that proclamation of the Gospel is an invitation. We do not impose; we propose. And in dialogue, we listen and we share what we believe, always seeking to go deeper in the common pursuit of truth. Just as in ecumenical activity the common basis for dialogue is a fundamental unity of faith, so in interreligious dialogue the common basis of our unity is the human family, and in more cases than not a belief in God. Each religion of the world is unique in its own way and has to be approached with this understanding.

However, it needs to be said that we have a particular relationship with Judaism that we have with no other religion. We cannot forget that Christianity was born from Judaism, and that it is where our roots remain. Abraham is our father in faith. The Pontifical Biblical Commission in its document *The Jewish People and Their Sacred Scriptures in the Christian Bible*, states "that the New Testament recognizes the authority of the Old Testament as divine revelation and that the New Testament cannot be properly understood apart from the Old Testament and the Jewish tradition which transmits it."[6] So we have a relationship that continues by reason of our origins in Jesus Christ—who was a devout Jew and the Anointed One of God (the Messiah, the Christ)—a relationship that is discontinuous since Christianity detached itself from Judaism as Christians were exiled from the synagogue; but this relationship must progress in new ways, since ultimately the Kingdom of God is one.

The Church also has a particular reason to be in relationship with Islam, since Christianity is a religion of Revelation, and Islam also identifies itself as such. While there has been longstanding hostility between Muslims and Christians, today, more than ever, there is a need for Catholic-Muslim dialogue. This can be done and is being done around the concept of revelation. Muslims can study the Bible; Christians can study the Qur'an.

I believe that one of the great days for the religions of the world occurred at Assisi in 1986 when the Holy Father led the World Day of Prayer for Peace. The Christian churches, ecclesial communities, Jews, and many religions of the world were represented in this prayer for peace. A just world, a world of peace, a world of right relations are all intimately connected to the coming of the Kingdom of God. Proclaiming the coming of the Kingdom and preparing for the Kingdom is a work of evangelization. It is not stretching the point to see interreligious dialogue and interreligious prayer as integral to the work of the new evangelization.

There are many important points to keep in mind as we seek to evangelize in an ecumenical and interreligious society. They are found in the living tradition of the Church, and we are guided in their use by the Magisterium. By way of conclusion, I would like to lift up three of these points.

First in importance is the centrality of prayer. Only through prayer will we be able to be faithful to the will of God and have the courage to persevere when the challenges seem insurmountable. At the meeting regarding *Christian Churches Together*, I had the opportunity to outline the ways we pray in the Catholic tradition. Representatives from the other faith family designations were able to do the same. What was said gave expression to our commonality and was truly complementary. After the panel presentation, we broke into interfaith groups, discussed prayer, and then prayed. One of the Evangelical ministers in our group said to me afterwards that he never thought he would be praying for a Catholic bishop by name and hear a Catholic bishop pray for him.

Second, even though dialogue is not evangelization, it is a most important means for evangelization in ecumenical and interreligious relations. The principles laid out in Paul VI's document *On the Church (Ecclesiam Suam)* remain compelling as the standard.[7]

Finally, we must keep in mind that the work of evangelization is the work of the Holy Spirit. The work of ecumenism is the work of the Holy Spirit. The work of interreligious relations is the work of the Holy Spirit. There is one Spirit who accomplishes all in all, just as there is one Lord and Savior, Jesus Christ, and one God, who is Father of all.

Bishop Stephen Blaire

A native of Los Angeles and the twelfth of fourteen children, Bishop Blair was ordained to the priesthood in 1967 for the Archdiocese of Los Angeles. After first serving as an associate pastor, he spent 1972 to 1986 in Catholic secondary education, mostly in administrative positions. In 1986 he was appointed moderator of the curia and chancellor of the archdiocese and in 1990, was ordained auxiliary bishop of Los Angeles. Bishop Blaire served as regional bishop of Our Lady of the Angels Pastoral Region from 1995 to 1999. In January 1999, he was appointed the fifth bishop of the Diocese of Stockton, California. He has served on many committees of the United States Conference of Catholic Bishops and is a former member of the Committee on Evangelization. He is currently the chairman of the Committee on Ecumenical and Interreligious Affairs.

NOTES

1 Paul VI, *On Evangelization in the Modern World* (*Evangelii Nuntiandi*) (Washington, DC: Libreria Editrice Vaticana–USCCB, 1975), no. 14.

2 John Paul II, *The Church in Europe* (*Ecclesia in Europa*) (Vatican City: Libreria Editrice Vaticana, June 28, 2003), no. 54.

3 John Paul II, *On the Permanent Validity of the Church's Missionary Mandate* (*Redemptoris Missio*) (Vatican City: Libreria Editrice Vaticana, December 7, 1990), no. 34.

4 Herbert Vorgrimler, general editor, *Commentary on the Documents of Vatican II* (New York: Herder and Herder, 1967). Also see. Paul VI, *Dogmatic Constitution on the Church* (*Lumen Gentium*) (Vatican City: Libreria Editrice Vaticana, November 21, 1964), no. 8.

5 John Paul II, *That They May Be One* (*Ut Unum Sint*) (Washington, DC: Libreria Editrice Vaticana–USCCB, 2001), no. 5, citing Congregation for the Doctrine of the Faith, *Letter to the Bishops of the Catholic Church on Some Aspects of the Church Understood as Communion* (*Communionis Notio*) (Vatican City: Libreria Editrice Vaticana, 28 May 1992), no. 4.

6 Pontifical Biblical Commission, *The Jewish People and Their Sacred Scriptures in the Christian Bible* (Vatican City: Libreria Editrice Vaticana, 2002), no. 1.

7 Paul VI, *On the Church* (*Ecclesiam Suam*) (Vatican City: Libreria Editrice Vaticana, August 6, 1964).

ECUMENICAL IMPLICATIONS FOR CATHOLIC EVANGELIZATION

Dr. Margaret Ralph

Good morning. I cannot begin to tell you how grateful and honored I am to be speaking with you today. As my talk unfolds and you hear the stories I will tell to illustrate my points regarding ecumenical implications for Catholic evangelization, I think you will come to realize just how heartfelt my gratitude is. For me, saying "yes" to the invitation to address this topic was more like saying "yes" to God then it was like saying "yes" to Fr. John Hurley. I don't mean the kind of "yes" that Jesus said in the agony in the garden; I mean the kind of "yes" you say with a high five. I would like to thank those who thought of having this meeting and planned it, because I think our conversations during the next three days are much needed and will be very important to our work.

I would like to tell you a little about my own background so that you can put my remarks in context. In terms of education, I am neither a theologian nor an ecumenist; I am an English major. I applied my knowledge of literary forms to Scripture and found myself working in the field of religious education. I have been secretary of educational ministries in the Diocese of Lexington, Kentucky, for sixteen years. Our office of Catholic education includes all parish-based religious education, youth ministry, family life ministry, and schools. Part of my job description is to be the direct service person for the Rite of Christian Initiation for Adults program (RCIA) and evangelization. My evangelization responsibilities account for my being with you today.

I have found it very helpful, in terms of promoting evangelization, to be in the office of Catholic education and to work routinely with the rest of the staff. As you probably know, the *General Directory for Catechesis* encourages us to see all of catechesis in the context of evangelization.[1] Catholic schools exist to evangelize the culture. So our diocesan organizational structure has lead to fruitful cooperation among us.

For those same sixteen years, I have been the director of two master of arts degree programs for Roman Catholics at Lexington Theological Seminary, a Disciples of Christ seminary. While this does not account for my deep interest in the ecumenical movement, it certainly does account for many of my ecumenical experiences, some of which I will be sharing with you today.

Catholic Identity

My responsibilities in both of these settings—the office of Catholic education and the seminary—have caused me to give a great deal of thought to the question of Catholic identity. For this reason, I was struck by this statement of Pope John Paul II in his magnificent encyclical *That They May Be One (Ut Unum Sint)*:

> It is absolutely clear that ecumenism, the movement promoting Christian unity, is not just some sort of "appendix" which is added to the Church's traditional activity. Rather, ecumenism is an organic part of her life and work, and consequently must pervade all that she is and does.[2]

In other words, being ecumenical is part of our Catholic identity. If we are not ecumenical, we are not living up to who we are supposed to be, not just because we are ecumenical officers, or evangelizers, or those who oversee our religious education programs, but also because we are baptized. Ecumenism is essential to our identity, and we are not yet paying anywhere near enough attention to it. This is why I am so grateful we have the opportunity to be in conversation on this topic with each other over the next three days.

I know that all of you who are directors of evangelization are well acquainted with the importance of giving witness, of telling our stories. In fact, the primary skill needed by an evangelizer is the ability to reflect on one's own life as a life in which God is powerful and present and then to give witness to that insight through story.

My own story leads me to believe that God has formed me to be an advocate for the importance of ecumenism in the life of every Catholic. I was raised in an ecumenical family. My father, Charles Nutting, was an English Republican Presbyterian; my mother, Mary Agnes Flannagan, was an Irish Democrat Roman Catholic. My parents loved each other, and they loved their three daughters.

My parents married during the time when the person who was not Catholic had to promise that the children of the marriage would be raised Catholic. My father made that promise, and he kept it. When I reached adulthood, I asked my father how difficult it had been for him to make such a promise. He told me that he did not think there was anything wrong with being Catholic. If he had thought that, he could not have made the promise. However, it had been extremely difficult for him because he knew that I would be taught that there was something wrong with being Presbyterian. To allow me to be taught such a thing was painful because my father came from a long line of Presbyterians; for at least seven generations, all of them were clergy or teachers. My father said it had been hard because he felt like he was turning his back on his ancestors.

My father's understanding that I would be taught that something was wrong with being Presbyterian turned out to be correct. I was taught that it was very sad that my father, because he was Presbyterian, would not make it to heaven. I remember as a child secretly praying for his conversion. I remember sneaking into my parents' bedroom and sprinkling holy water on his pillow. When I look back on all of this now, I think that my father must have been praying that I would someday understand that what I had been taught was wrong. His prayers were obviously stronger than mine because I am the one who has been converted, along with the Church that planted such an idea in my head in the first place.

I now have the opportunity to travel all over the country to teach Scripture. As I have gone from place to place, I have learned that before the Second Vatican Council, many Catholics were taught to avoid other Christian churches like the plague. Catholics could not attend a worship service in a Protestant church. Some were even told to cross the street if they had to pass a Protestant church, just to be a little further away from it. If you were not subjected to this kind of teaching yourself, it may be hard to believe that others were. So I would like to take just a minute or so and have you turn to the person next to you to see what that person's experience has been. Were you taught prejudice or not?

If we have been taught prejudice, it is difficult to outgrow it. I realize that all of our conversions are ongoing. However, I am still somewhat in awe about how hard it is to realize that something you thought to be true is, in fact, false. I think I was fortunate in that the very institution in whose authority I had placed so much trust—and which taught me a deep-seeded prejudice—was the institution that called me to conversion. Thank God for the Second Vatican Council!

I was at St. Mary's College in South Bend, Indiana, while the Second Vatican Council was taking place. I remember clearly that a speaker came to the college to inform us about the wonderful ecumenical progress that was being made. The speaker was talking about the importance of ecumenical dialogue. He said that our posture, when it comes to ecumenical dialogue, cannot be, "I am right and you are wrong." I raised my hand, and in front of God and everybody I asked, "How can our posture be anything else since we are right and they are wrong?"

I obviously had a lot to learn from the Second Vatican Council's *Decree on Ecumenism*, which tells us that "there can be no ecumenism worthy of the name without interior conversion."[3] Isn't that the truth!

Basic Principles

The topic I have been asked to address is "Ecumenical Implications for Catholic Evangelization." However, before I address that topic directly, I would like to define terms and state basic principles since it is possible that those of you who are directors of evangelization may not be familiar with ecumenical documents, and that those of you who are ecumenical officers may not be familiar with evangelization documents.

The introduction to the Second Vatican Council's *Decree on Ecumenism* gives us the theological basis for Catholic involvement in the ecumenical movement. It says:

> The restoration of unity among all Christians is one of the principal concerns of the Second Vatican Council. Christ the Lord founded one Church and one Church only. However, many Christian communions present themselves to men as the true inheritors of Jesus Christ; all indeed profess to be followers of the Lord but they differ in mind and go their different ways, as if Christ himself were divided. Certainly, such division openly contradicts the will of Christ, scandalizes the world, and damages that most holy cause, the preaching of the Gospel to every creature.[4]

The United States Conference of Catholic Bishops' document on evangelization *Go and Make Disciples* defines evangelization as "bringing the Good News of Jesus into every human situation and seeking to convert individuals and society by the divine power of the Gospel itself."[5] It is evangelization that suffers as long as our divisions remain.

How serious a problem do we have if our efforts to evangelize are hampered? We have a very serious problem. Why? Because the Church exists to evangelize. As Paul VI wrote in *On Evangelization in the Modern World* (*Evangelii Nuntiandi*), "Evangelizing is in fact the grace and vocation proper to the Church, her deepest identity. She exists in order to evangelize."[6] Since the Church exists to evangelize, and her efforts to evangelize are crippled until Christian churches reunite, all of us—ecumenical officers and directors of evangelization—are partners in helping every Roman Catholic realize that we must be ecumenical and that we must evangelize in order to be truly Catholic. Ours are not offices with borders as far as our responsibilities go. Rather, our efforts need to be like leaven in the bread. We, ecumenical officers and directors of evangelization both, in order to fulfill our missions, must affect the whole loaf, the whole Church.

In addition to the *Decree on Ecumenism*, the Second Vatican Council gave us *The Dogmatic Constitution on the Church*. Here we read that Christ's one Church "subsists in the Catholic Church, which is governed by the successor of Peter and by the Bishops in communion with him, although many elements of sanctification and of truth are found outside of its visible structure." (I will say more on this later.)[7] The *Catechism of the Catholic Church*, in summing up the teaching from these two documents, says, "Christ's Spirit uses these Churches and ecclesial communities as means of salvation."[8] The good news here is that my father is obviously going to a high place in heaven.

All three of the ecumenical documents that I have quoted affirm that Christ established only one Church, and that those who are baptized into Christ's Body are members of that Church. Although I had read this truth many times, the ramifications of these statements did not sink in for many years. About eighteen years ago, I was able to take one giant step forward when I was an adult-education consultant for the Diocese of Covington. At that time, the Kentucky Council of Churches was offering a series of workshops on the World Council of Churches document *Baptism, Eucharist, and Ministry*.[9] I was invited to attend the workshop series. One of the speakers said that when we pray for the unity of the Church, we should not pray for unity, because we already have that: there is one Body of Christ; there is one Church. We should pray for visible unity—that we learn how to live so that the unity we already have becomes visible.

This statement struck me as profoundly true. The *Catechism of the Catholic Church* sums up our unity in its paragraph no. 813:

> The Church is one because of her source: "the highest exemplar and source of this mystery is the unity, in the Trinity of Persons, of one God, the Father and the Son in the Holy Spirit."
>
> The Church is one because of her founder: for "the Word made flesh, the prince of peace, reconciled all men to God by the cross, . . . restoring the unity of all in one people and one body."

The Church is one because of her "soul": "It is the Holy Spirit, dwelling in those who believe and pervading and ruling over the entire Church, who brings about that wonderful communion of the faithful."

Unity is of the essence of the Church.

Since hearing that workshop speaker, I have prayed daily for full visible unity among Christians. I also have found it extremely painful, as a person involved in the ecumenical movement, to act in ways that give witness to our divisions rather than to our unity.

This leads me to the topic of how we Roman Catholics who want to promote church unity should act in ecumenical settings. As I mentioned earlier, one of my great privileges is to be on the faculty of Lexington Theological Seminary. About sixteen years ago (before the Diocese of Lexington was born), the Diocese of Covington formed a partnership with the Disciples of Christ Seminary in order to offer the possibility of graduate study to our parish directors of religious education. While participating in conversations about establishing this partnership, I learned that the Disciples of Christ did not start out to become a denomination. Rather, they were founded to promote ecumenism. They exist to try to heal the divisions in Christ's Body, the Church. The seminary invited the diocese to add specifically Catholic courses to the curriculum and jointly to select the person who would teach these courses.

My involvement with the seminary has forced me to define how I should act in ecumenical settings. This has sometimes been difficult for me because I find our churches' lack of visible unity so painful. I find it difficult to refrain from participating in the Eucharist, especially since I am invited to do so. I want to be faithful to the instructions in the *Directory for the Application of Principles and Norms on Ecumenism*, which explains that, since receiving the Eucharist together is a sign of unity achieved, and since we have not yet achieved that unity, we should refrain from celebrating the Eucharist together with "ministers of other Churches or ecclesial Communities."[11] You have likely found yourself in similar situations, perhaps at family weddings or funerals. So before I move on to discuss how I have come to deal with this issue, I would like to ask you to turn to the person next to you and discuss when and how you personally have felt the pain of religious division and how you have chosen to act in regard to it.

One of my sons, who is a psychologist, told me a joke that has helped me deal with my discomfort when my actions witness to our lack of unity rather than to our unity. Picture a psychologist sitting in his office talking to a patient. The psychologist says to the patient, "You know, we have met for an hour a week for a year now and it is always about you, you, you."

You might wonder what this joke has to do with the topic at hand. As a Catholic working for the visible unity of the Church, I am not like the patient talking to the psychologist. In that setting, I would expect the focus to be on my personal feelings. But that is not at all the case in my work as a person longing for the Church's unity. It is true that I experience a good deal of pain when I act in ways that witness to our division. However, my feelings are not anywhere near the most important consideration. I am choosing to act in such a way that I am giving witness to the present position of my own Church on questions such as sharing Communion. The goal is not that I, individually, will express this union that we all desire, but that our churches will express this union. In other words, ecumenism is not about "me, me, me," or about "you, you, you," or about any one individual. It is about our churches' corporately being in dialogue, reaching mutual understandings, and learning how to live out the unity that we know is God's will.

The goal of the ecumenical movement is that all churches be able to gather around one Eucharistic table. The hope is that if we each center ourselves on Jesus Christ, and if we dialogue lovingly with each other, we will each experience the degree of conversion necessary for us to celebrate the Eucharist together in truth and love. We no longer take the position that blame for our divisions belongs entirely to the Protestant churches (those who protested), and that the road to unity lies in their coming back home. This posture, in which only "those other people" are called to conversion of heart, reminds me of the title of a book I once saw that was something like *We Could Have a Great Relationship If It Weren't for You*. Rather, we acknowledge fault on all sides and call ourselves, as well as others, to conversion.

The ecumenical movement has many practical implications for Catholic evangelization. I have already tried to address or model three of these implications. They are

• The need for a deep personal conversion for those of us who were taught prejudice against our brother and sister Christians

- The need to witness to our own experience as one tool of dialogue

- The need to familiarize ourselves with our Church documents so that we become knowledgeable about where we are ecumenically

I will now name some more implications that I have experienced in the course of my work in order to spur your thinking, but I am sure that you will be able to add to this list based on your own experience.

Guidelines for Dialogue

In order to participate in ecumenism, we need to learn how to enter into dialogue with other Christians. Dialogue can be formal or informal, but certain guidelines help immensely in making the dialogue fruitful in terms of moving toward visible unity. For three years, I had the great honor of participating in the national dialogue between Roman Catholics and United Methodists. It was our goal to produce a resource that would help bring ecumenical dialogue to the person in the pew. Our dialogue resulted in a resource entitled *Yearning to Be One* that was published jointly by the United States Catholic Conference and Discipleship Resources.[12] The guidelines for dialogue that we name in that resource are based on guidelines written by Michael Kinnamon in his book *Truth and Community: Diversity and Its Limits in the Ecumenical Movement*.[13] I had the great good fortune to work with Dr. Kinnamon because he was dean at Lexington Theological Seminary for many years.

As I share these guidelines with you, I will also name a ramification for each guideline that I have discovered in my own ecumenical involvement. I encourage you to think about the ramifications these guidelines would have in your local ministry settings.

Ecumenical dialogue must have a spiritual orientation. A willingness to be transformed is essential. One ramification of this guideline is that people who are positive that they are already the recipients of the whole truth and who have as a goal to convert others to their way of thinking are not yet ready for ecumenical dialogue. The union of churches will involve new insights and mea culpas on everyone's part. We all have something to learn.

In ecumenical dialogue, participants must be given permission to define themselves, to describe and witness to the faith in their own terms. One ramification of this guideline is that those involved in ecumenical dialogue have to learn to listen so that they do not impose on

18

others what they have been told that others believe. For instance, the fact that a person is not Roman Catholic and does not use the word "transubstantiation" does not necessarily mean that the person does not believe that Christ is present in the Eucharist.

In order to be helpful to the group in an interdenominational dialogue, each participant needs to have a clear understanding of his or her own faith and to present it with honesty and sincerity. A ramification of this guideline is that our parish adult-education programs need to do more than pass on the truths of our faith, which is the "bottom line." We need to offer adult education programs that honor the experience of adults and encourage critical thinking so participants not only can name the truths of our faith, but also understand, believe, and live out those truths.

The integrity of each person must be treasured by everyone. As each person speaks, he or she must be mindful not only of his or her own integrity but also of the integrity of the person with whom he or she may be disagreeing. The desired fruit is mutual growth, not victory. One ramification of this guideline that I myself took years to learn is that the goal of dialogue is not to persuade our dialogue partners to become Roman Catholic. When others speak, we are to listen not with a goal of telling them where their thinking is flawed, but rather, with appreciation for their insights. We all have a great deal to learn.

Remember that dialogue, particularly at the congregational level, is between people and not just between churches or ideological positions. One ramification of this guideline is that we have to learn to listen with deep respect to each person. Often we think we know what a person thinks when we know that person's denomination. Our presuppositions may not turn out to be accurate.

Keep the dialogue in the present. Participants do not need to represent or defend their faith communion throughout history. Present issues are the ones that need to be discussed. One ramification of this guideline for me is gratitude. I do not want to take responsibility for or to defend the Crusades or the Church's treatment of Galileo.

Be willing to separate essentials from nonessentials. This guideline once again emphasizes the importance of good adult education. If Catholics do not understand the hierarchy of truths—that is, the relationship of core truths to truths that are derived from those core truths—they will find ecumenical dialogue beyond them.

Do not insist on more agreement from your partners in dialogue than you would expect from members of your own faith communion. I cannot but smile when I think about this guideline. In my own diocese and (I think) in many dioceses, there are often alarming divisions among Roman Catholics. For instance, our Roman Catholic Church teaches us to be contextualists, not fundamentalists, when reading Scripture. When I teach the contextualist approach to Scripture to Catholic adults, I often run in to severe criticism. My colleagues at the seminary who are not Roman Catholic are all contextualists in their approach to Scripture. Much more agreement on this subject exists at the seminary than in the parish. If the level of agreement among Catholics is our measure of an acceptable degree of unity with other Christians, then we must be closer to our goal than we realize.

Interpret the faith of your dialogue partner in its best light, rather than in its worst. I think we can all understand the importance of this guideline. For example, I would describe myself as completely pro-life. However, I am embarrassed by some of the strategies that some of my fellow pro-life Catholics employ, and I certainly do not want to be associated with a person who would blow up an abortion clinic. Every religious group has its fanatics, and it is not right to judge a group by its least admirable representatives.

Do not avoid hard issues. You undoubtedly will not want to tackle these issues first; but once trust has been established, it is important to discuss even difficult issues. For me, inter-communion is such an issue. I am hesitant to tell others that I do not recognize the ordination of their ministers and that this makes their Eucharist questionable in my eyes. However, in discussing this issue, I learned more about my own beliefs and how Catholic teaching appears to others. It was certainly an enlightening conversation. (I will say more about this later.)

Search for ways to turn the increased understanding achieved through dialogue into activities for renewal. An immediate way to accomplish that is to have it lead to prayer. But as time goes on, other actions will occur to the group. Shared ecumenical outreach activities are an excellent way to promote ecumenical understanding. Small faith-sharing groups are another. In my own diocese, we also have pulpit exchanges, ecumenical "sister" churches, and ecumenical ministerial associations. The more we work and pray together, the more we will grow in our love and understanding of each other (Kinnamon, 27).

Each of these guidelines has many practical ramifications of its own that I have not named. However, I hope that you will take these guidelines to heart and think about how they might inform not only your dialogues with others, but also many aspects of your life as Catholic evangelizers and ecumenists.

How We Are Perceived by Others

Another ecumenical implication for Catholic evangelization is that we need to learn, without being defensive, how others perceive us. I have had a number of sobering experiences in this regard, and I would like to tell you about two of them. The first experience occurred during the sessions held by the Kentucky Council of Churches on the *Baptist, Eucharist, and Ministry* (BEM) document. I was part of a painful and enlightening dialogue.

The Kentucky Council of Churches held three ongoing education weekends not only to acquaint us with BEM, but to also have us struggle with it. Efforts were fruitful in this regard. This is what happened: During the weekend devoted to Eucharist, we celebrated a "Lima Liturgy." For those of you not familiar with the Lima Liturgy, it is a celebration of the Eucharist put together by ecumenists, with the goal of expressing our unity to the greatest degree possible. I was attending this gathering at the invitation of the Diocese of Covington, and I was instructed to attend the Lima Liturgy but to refrain from receiving Eucharist. As it happened, the celebrant at the liturgy was my father's pastor from the Presbyterian Church in Lexington. My father admired this man very much.

After the liturgy, we gathered to discuss how we had experienced the liturgy, what we had chosen to do, and how we had felt about it. I did not have the courage to say anything. However, a Catholic priest wearing a Roman collar stood up and said, "I did not receive Eucharist. The reason is that I do not recognize the validity of the ordination of a Presbyterian minister. Therefore it was not clear to me that what we were celebrating was Eucharist."

This priest expressed exactly what I had been taught. However, there was an audible groan throughout the room. Then a person I did not know stood up and said, "You Catholics make me so angry with all you have done to fracture the Body of Christ with stands like we just heard. However, I am Baptist, and every time I think about just how angry I am, I remind myself what we Baptists have done when it comes to Baptism." This comment was met with stunned silence. I did not understand what was happening. I turned to the person next to me, who knew I am Roman Catholic, and asked, "What does he mean?" That person said, "From his point of view, you are not baptized because your Baptism was not by immersion." I was stunned beyond words. How could anyone think that I am not baptized? My whole life flows from and gives witness to my Baptism. However, I still did not say anything because I realized that my father's minister might ask me, "How can anyone think I am not ordained? My whole life flows from and gives witness to my ordination."

My second sobering ecumenical experience again involved the Eucharist. I went to a "Serendipity" workshop in Indianapolis. The *Serendipity Bible* is an edition of the Bible that has discussion questions in the margins for faith-sharing groups. I believe it was developed by Presbyterians.[14] Over one thousand people attended the workshop, and if there were other Roman Catholics, I did not meet them. One of the speakers, as a side comment, mentioned that an elder in the Presbyterian Church could preside at the Eucharist. I was interested in this comment because my father had been an elder. To my knowledge, he had never presided at a Eucharist, although he was very active in his church. To make sure I had heard correctly, I turned to the person next to me and asked, "Did you hear what he just said?" She said, "Yes, but there's no explaining it." I said, "I want to make sure I heard him correctly. Would

---

The Lord gave us a message that is unique. All faiths are not merely different versions of the same thing. Knowing Christ Jesus and belonging to his Church are not the same as believing anything else and belonging to any other community. Pope John Paul II has pointed out, "While acknowledging that God loves all people and grants them the possibility of being saved (cf. 1 Tm 2:4), the Church believes that God has established Christ as the one mediator and that she herself has been established as the universal sacrament of salvation."

—*Go and Make Disciples: A National Plan and Strategy for Catholic Evangelization in the United States* (Washington, DC: USCCB, 2002), no. 32.

---

you mind telling me what you heard?" She said, "Well, there's no explaining it, but some of these churches organize themselves so that only one special person can preside at Eucharist, and if that person isn't there, well, you just can't have Eucharist. There's just no explaining it." I have no words to describe the effect these words had on me, but they helped me in several other settings.

One day at the seminary, we had an interfaith convocation on the Eucharist so that we would all understand each other and examine why we were choosing to act as we were. Later, a woman who had worshipped in a Disciples of Christ church all her life came up to me and said, "I'm in my thirties, and this is the first time in my life that I have realized that some churches can't have Eucharist unless an ordained person is present." I said, "Well, don't feel too bad. I was in my forties before I realized that in some churches a person need not be ordained to preside at Eucharist."

Another issue regarding the way people of other religions perceive us is that we need to learn to word things in a way that is understandable, so that a person does not have to be a theologian to understand what we are talking about. Earlier we referred to the *Dogmatic Constitution on the Church*, and its statement that Christ's one Church "subsists in the Catholic Church." The average person in the pew does not know what "subsists in" means or how significant it is that the statement says that Christ's one Church "subsists in the Catholic Church" (no. 8) rather than saying, "Christ's one Church is the Catholic Church."

In trying to explain that we do not think "one Church is as good as another," many Catholics still speak of the Catholic Church as the "one true Church," thus seeming to deny that Christ does use other churches as means of salvation.

I heard an evangelizer who is probably well known to many of you, Fr. Bruce Neili, explain this truth in language that everyone could understand and that did not put down other churches. Of course, he did this with an Italian flare that I lack, but I am sure you will still appreciate his point. He said, "I think of our beloved Catholic Church as a pizza supreme. Now, some people love pepperoni, some mushrooms, some extra cheese. And, of course, all pizza is delicious. But the Catholic Church is pizza supreme. We have all the means of salvation. There is something here for everyone!" Notice that, he said, "All pizza is delicious." In giving witness to our own understanding of the truth, we must find ways to speak our truth in love without seeming to deny or dismiss the expression of truth held dear by others.

The Rite of Christian Initiation of Adults

I do not know how many of you who are diocesan directors of evangelization also have responsibility for the Rite of Christian Initiation of Adults (RCIA). In our diocese, I have direct responsibility for both. My work in RCIA has taught me additional ecumenical implications for Catholic evangelization. When we began implementing the RCIA process in the 1980s, we did not do a good job of making a clear distinction between candidates and catechumens, that is, between baptized Christians who were coming into full communion with the Roman Catholic Church and those who were not baptized.

I remember an occasion many years ago when I was the sponsor for a candidate in our home parish. We were celebrating the Rite of Acceptance. As I made the sign of the cross on the candidate's forehead, ears, lips, hands, and feet, she had tears streaming down her cheeks. Afterward I said to her, "I could see that you found this ceremony very moving. I did too." She replied, "I found it very insulting." I was dumbfounded. Finally I said, "Please tell me why you felt insulted. I really need to know." She said, "I've been Christian all my life. The words of that ceremony didn't honor my experience at all." I have never forgotten her gift to me.

We must be careful always to make a clear distinction between candidates and catechumens at every stage of the Rite. For instance, the scrutinies are worded for the unbaptized. Candidates should not celebrate the scrutinies as though they are catechumens. The dismissal for "breaking open the word" is meant for catechumens. Here again, a clear distinction should be made between candidates and catechumens. In our diocese, during our first celebration of the Rite of Election and the Call to Continuing Conversion when we called the candidates, we named the Christian traditions that they were bringing with them. We meant this to be an affirmation of the richness of their backgrounds. However, when we asked people how they experienced the Rite, some had experienced that naming of other denominations as triumphalism. Since that was not our intent, we have not continued that practice. Instead our bishop has simply affirmed and thanked the candidates for the rich gifts that their past experiences will be for us.

The Catholic Approach to Scripture

One more ecumenical implication for Catholic evangelization involves our Catholic approach to Scripture. This is the area in which I have done most of my work, and it is close to my heart. The Catholic Church teaches us to be biblical contextualists. We are to consider the literary form of the book or story in which a passage appears, the beliefs of the time when the passage was written, and how this passage fits into a two-thousand-year process of Revelation before we claim to understand the truth that an inspired biblical author is teaching.

I call this contextualist approach to the Bible the Catholic Church's approach to the Bible because it is the method of biblical interpretation that our Church teaches us to use.[15] However, the disagreement about how to understand the Revelation that Scripture teaches us is not an interdenominational disagreement, but rather, a disagreement within denominations. Many adult Roman Catholics do not know that our Church teaches us to be contextualists, rather than fundamentalists. The reasons for this lack of knowledge are that the contextualist approach can only be taught to a person whose cognitive development is that of an adult (in most cases, not until a person is a junior in high school), and that our Catholic Church has not done a good job of providing adult education. This lack of biblical understanding has ramifications for both ecumenists and evangelizers.

Many of the negative associations that people have with the word "evangelization" are the result of the way some evangelizers abuse Scripture. I am sure we all still remember the way Scripture was abused as the new millennium approached a few years ago. You are probably also aware of the popularity of the Left Behind series of books. In both instances, a fundamentalist approach to Scripture resulted in the use of apocalyptic passages from the Bible to frighten people rather than to offer them hope, the latter of which is what the original authors had intended.

It is crucial that, as evangelizers and as ecumenists, we act in fidelity to our contextualist approach to Scripture. I would like to give you two examples of instances in which I have seen Catholics fail to do this in regard to topics that are of current importance to all of us, evangelizers and ecumenists. In each instance, I want to make it clear that I am not challenging the teaching of the Catholic Church. However, I am challenging the idea that, in our evangelizing or ecumenical activities, we can use the Bible to "proof text" that our teaching is correct.

The question of the ordination of women is an area of ecumenical disagreement. I have often heard our Church's teaching against the ordination of women explained with the comment, "Jesus ordained only men."

This argument is not faithful to what the Catholic Church teaches about Scripture. We are not to use a passage of Scripture to answer a question that the original author was not addressing. When those who disagree with this teaching respond, "Jesus did not ordain anyone," we are left in a weakened position because it is true that Jesus did not ordain anyone.

A second example is the question of gay unions, a subject that is causing disagreement not only between denominations, but also within them. Again, let me remind you that I am not challenging the Catholic Church's clear teaching that sexual activity between people of the same sex is wrong. However, it does not add strength to the Roman Catholic position to say that Scripture clearly teaches against committed gay relationships. Biblical authors certainly condemn unnatural acts committed in lust (see Rom 1:24-27). But they never consider or discuss the question of sexual orientation. We cannot be faithful to our own tradition and, at the same time, use out-of-context biblical passages to prove that we are right in regard to teachings that biblical authors were not addressing.

We are good contextualists when it comes to deciding whether or not it is moral to earn interest on our loans, when we argue against slavery and the death penalty, and even when we acknowledge that the world is round. Let us not explain our teaching on important current issues by failing to live up to our own teaching on the proper way to interpret the Bible.

One Last Story

As I conclude my remarks, I would like to tell one more story. This story is about a gift that God gave my mother on the occasion of my father's death. My father had given me instructions about how to arrange his funeral in the Presbyterian Church. He wanted one of two clergy persons to preside, both of whom he admired. One had moved away. The other was someone whom I thought might not be suitable.

Several years before my father's death, this minister came to me and told me over several weeks of meetings that she shared the Catholic Church's beliefs regarding the true presence of Christ in the Eucharist, that the Presbyterian Church celebrated Eucharist only four times a year, and that she would like to receive Eucharist in our Church. She asked me if that would be possible. I referred her to the person who was our diocesan ecumenical officer at that time. After conversations with her and with the pope's representative in Washington, D.C., it was determined that she could receive Eucharist in our Church as long as it did not cause scandal. Some time later, she reached retirement age as a Presbyterian minister, and after her retirement, she came into full visible unity with the Roman Catholic Church. That is why I thought she might not be acceptable now as a presider at my father's funeral.

Several weeks before my father died, we had an ecumenical study day for pastoral leaders in our diocese. Our bishop at that time invited me to attend because he knew of my deep interest in ecumenism. The leaders of other denominations also were invited. I sat down next to a person whom I did not know and introduced myself. It turned out that my companion was the head of the Presbyterians. It was not long before my dilemma regarding my father's funeral came pouring out. I explained the whole situation and then said, "I imagine it would not be appropriate for me to ask the minister who is now Catholic to preside at the funeral." He said, "I wouldn't have a problem with it." I could not believe my ears.

However, that is the way it worked out. At my father's funeral, as we sat in the Second Presbyterian Church, I turned to my mother and said, "Do you see that minister? She is a Roman Catholic. I think this is God's way of telling you that you and Dad belonged to Christ's one Church all these years and that Dad is now safe in God's hands."

My life experience has left me with a dream and a question, both of which I offer you. The dream is this: I dream of a day when all Christians are gathered around one Eucharistic table. I believe this is already occurring at the heavenly banquet. My Irish Catholic ancestors and my English Presbyterian ancestors are not experiencing the divisions that we are still experiencing here on earth.

My question is this: After years of thinking about the scandal of our divisions and of experiencing the pain that these divisions cause, I find myself asking, "Why is agreement rather than love the goal we must reach in order to express our unity?" In my family we did not agree, but we did and do love each other. I think that love is ultimately the bond of unity.

Now you have heard my story. I hope, that as our time together continues, we will have opportunities to hear each other's stories. I am confident that our day spent discussing the ecumenical implications for Catholic evangelization will help us grow in our ability to serve the Church, the whole Body of Christ, as baptized people called to be both evangelizers and ecumenists.

Dr. Margaret Ralph

Dr. Margaret Ralph is the secretary of educational ministries and director of evangelization and RCIA in the Diocese of Lexington, Kentucky. She directs two master's degree programs for Roman Catholics at Lexington Theological Seminary, a Disciples of Christ seminary, and she has been a participant in the Roman Catholic–United Methodist national dialogue.

NOTES

1 Vatican Congregation for the Clergy, *General Directory for Catechesis* (Washington, DC: Libreria Editrice Vaticana–USCCB, 1997).

2 John Paul II, *That They May Be One (Ut Unum Sint)* (Washington, DC: Libreria Editrice Vaticana–USCCB, 2001), no. 20.

3 Second Vatican Council, *Decree on Ecumenism (Unitatis Redintegratio)* in *Vatican Council II—New Revised Edition: The Conciliar and Post Conciliar Documents* 2, Austin Flannery, ed. (Collegeville, MN: The Liturgical Press, 1992), no. 7.

4 *Decree on Ecumenism*, no. 1.

5 United States Conference of Catholic Bishops, *Go and Make Disciples: A National Plan and Strategy for Catholic Evangelization in the United States.* Tenth Anniversary English and Spanish Edition (Washington, DC: USCCB, 2002), no. 10.

6 Paul VI, *On Evangelization in the Modern World {Evangelii Nuntiandi)* (Washington, DC: USCCB, 1999), no. 14.

7 Second Vatican Council, *Dogmatic Constitution on the Church (Lumen Gentium)* in Austin Flannery, ed., *Vatican Council II—New Revised Edition: The Conciliar and Post Conciliar Documents* 2 (Collegeville, MN: The Liturgical Press, 1992), no. 8.

8 Libreria Editrice Vaticana, *Catechism of the Catholic Church*, 2nd ed. (Washington, DC: Libreria Editrice Vaticana–USCCB, 2000), no. 819.

9 *Baptism, Eucharist, and Ministry* (Geneva: World Council of Churches, 1982).

10 *Catechism*, no. 813.

11 Pontifical Council for Promoting Christian Unity, *Directory for the Application of Principles and Norms on Ecumenism* (Washington, DC: USCCB, 1995), no. 104.

12 *Yearning to Be One: Spiritual Dialogue Between Catholics and United Methodists* (Nashville: Discipleship Resources and Washington, DC: USCCB, 2000).

13   Michael Kinnamon, *Truth and Community: Diversity and Its Limits in the Ecumenical Movement.* (Grand Rapids, MI: W. B. Eerdmans Publishing, 1988), 29-32.

14 *Serendipity Bible for Groups: New International Version* (Littleton, CO: Serendipity House, 1988).

15 *Catechism*, nos. 110 and 112.

JEWISH RELATIONS
AND CATHOLIC EVANGELIZATION

FR. ARTHUR L. KENNEDY

As is true of so many other aspects of the Second Vatican Council, the teaching and developments in 1965 *Declaration on the Relation of the Church to Non-Christian Religions* (*Nostra Aetate*) (NA) are simultaneously old and new. They are old in the sense that there is a long history of Church teaching about religions other than Christianity, as well as substantive theological reflection on the mystery of Israel and the divine election of the Jewish people beginning with Abraham and stretching through all the prophets. The document's teachings and developments are also new in the sense that the contexts have changed and the theological substance is now brought forth into a public ecclesiastical teaching of the mystery of divine life and the mystery of the people of Israel as being foundational to the mystery of the Church.[1]

First, it is helpful to consider briefly what the older, or classical, teachings were, and then to consider what the modern insights are into natural religion and the mystery of Israel and Judaism. Such considerations will give a broad context both to the advances of the Second Vatican Council and to the topic of this reflection.

Natural Religion

On the matter of religion and its meaning, it was the ancient teaching of the Catholic Church that religion was one of the most important of the natural virtues. While the sources and meaning of the term "religion" differed (relegere: to attend to carefully; religere: to recover [God]; and religare: to bind to [God]), the last of these meanings was the one accepted by Christian thinkers in the ancient and medieval world.[2]

In the modern world, the teachings and insights of the Second Vatican Council—not only in Nostra Aetate but also in a wide variety of the Council's constitutions and decrees—were prepared over many decades by the studies of biblical, patristic, and systematic theologians; historians; philosophers; and cultural anthropologists. As a result of

31

such advances in understanding, the meaning of "religion" as "natural virtue" was given a new context. As a virtue, religion came to be recognized in different cultures as an experience of God, a recognition that was expressed in symbols and in myths that articulated how humans came into being, how they related to the divinity, and how they were to order both personal and communal spiritual life.

A beginning of the modern sense of history was formulated at the end of the eighteenth century and beginning of the nineteenth century. While the first study of cultures that recognized them as having their unique characteristics was written about in the mid-nineteenth century, sociology was initiated by Auguste Comte in the 1830s, and it was immediately appropriated and improved upon by the great French Catholic sociologist Frederic LePlay in the 1840s.[3]

Philosophical phenomenology—particularly in the writings of Edmund Husserl and Max Scheler—developed in the early twentieth century, providing new insights about the activity and order of human consciousness and the place of symbols and myths in humans' grasping of meaning and truth. Scriptural studies, liturgical studies, patristic research, and a fuller systematic and symbolic theology began in the 1880s and rose to new heights in the 1920s and 1930s.[4] All of these areas of knowledge had begun to deepen the Church's awareness and knowledge of the mystery that is already present in its founding by the Lord Jesus. Similarly, a fuller understanding of other religions and of the Church's relation to them arose.

The Jewish Religion

Throughout her history, the Church has drawn upon developing secular insights that permit her a deeper comprehension of some aspect of the total mystery that is revealed to her and that constitutes her. Often, by removing the human ideologies that may have brought forth these developments, the Church purifies the original insights and thus is able to find the beneficial images, metaphors, and analogies that offer a fuller and more differentiated understanding of the divine wisdom within the Revelation. This is what she did in the appropriation of the philosophical differentiations that came with the Greek Gentile converts of the Patristic Age; similarly, she developed a systematic specialization in the medieval age after the discovery of the writings of Aristotle; and again in the Renaissance with a reappropriation of the texts and meanings of the ancient classics. At present, the Church is again engaged in bringing the insights from the secular social sciences developed through the nineteenth and twentieth centuries to assist in grasping more deeply the mystery of her nature.

The Church had an early understanding of Judaism through Scripture and liturgy; through the Incarnation of the Word; through the Blessed Virgin Mary; through her unique bond mediated by our Lord in his life, death, and Resurrection; through his election of the Twelve; through her living in close proximity with Jewish communities in Jerusalem; and through the forms of her earliest teaching, as the Didache.5 In addition, there were many accounts and reflections made by patristic theologians and other theologians who were engaged in developing the systematic turn in Christian thought in the medieval period.

It is clearly important that the God of Israel is not a natural deity, but rather, the supernatural God who is revealed in the writings of the Hebrew Scriptures and in the historical living of the Jewish people.6 The writings continually point to the slow and unsteady development of the people in their relationship with God, through the struggle for fidelity to their covenant. The absolute fidelity of God—who is the Creator of all things and the One who watches over the people who are coming into being—is seen over and against the failings of the people.

But the failings do not prevent the God of Israel from a purpose that is always a mystery. Christians know this first through their reading of Hebrew Scriptures, and then through their finding of the flow of the Jewish people's history in their own. The Church's fathers reflected on the meanings of Scripture and developed modes of interpretation for allowing the mystery that was being revealed to guide their understanding.

St. Augustine carefully drew on the relationships of the New Testament teachings to Hebrew Scriptures and recognized patterns of fulfillment that recur over and over in Hebrew Scriptures. But the more systematic writings of St. Thomas Aquinas, both his biblical commentaries and his Summa Theologica, reveal a consistent unfolding of the meaning of "fulfillment" in its particular expressions in both the Hebrew Scriptures and the New Testament. This pattern of Revelation, common to the whole of Scripture, is of considerable importance for Christian understanding. The Hebrew Scriptures' theme of God's unique action in both Revelation and the historical experience of the Jewish people is shown by Aquinas to be the same activity that occurs in the person of Christ. [7]

As is true regarding her knowledge of and relationship to other religions, the Church has drawn on modern intelligence and has sought a deeper understanding of the mystery of Judaism. This modern understanding was underway before the political rise of Nazism and the horror of the *Shoah*. However, the memory of the *Shoah* rightly requires profound new responses, especially in our considerations of the Church's evangelical mission and Judaism.

Before we consider some of the new insights the Church has into her relation with Judaism and her theological insights from the Second Vatican Council, let us briefly consider—as we did on the matter of natural religions—insights drawn from modern secular studies.

In modern intellectual developments, important insights have emerged within secular fields of study about the origins of the Jewish experience of God as a completely different reality from that of all the surrounding religions at the time. For the most part, early and higher natural religions were cosmogonic. That is to say, they read the divine as a transcendent cosmic order "out there," and they proceeded to develop symbols for shaping their world to attune it to the cosmic order. Some persons living within the cosmogonic societies were assumed to be able to participate in the cosmic eternal order and escape the fate of suffering and death upon earth. The knowledge humans had of the struggles and fears of life was enormous, and this created a tension that led to a quest for symbolizing those relationships that were considered divine, cosmic, and personal. Thus, symbols of participation recognized a wide range of different beings, and these symbols simultaneously grasped the "aloneness" and transience of human existence: that is, one man lasts while another passes away; societies outlast their members; societies pass while the world lasts.

The symbols expressed what people sensed to be a hierarchy of existence by distinguishing those beings that were transient from those that endured or had eternal being. Within this experience was a desire to be in attunement with what endured and to transcend the transience that humans knew.

The unseen God became the model for organizing ordinary human society, for formulating the symbols, and for the systematic thinking of philosophers and theologians (as in Babylonia, Assyria, and Egypt). There came into human imagination and language a quest for something that saved one from the "going-out" of existence by one's sharing in a divine cosmic existence. And thus, the people sought to be attuned to the cycles of nature as enduring beings, and in this mode of a fated existence, they shaped the order of their societies and cultures.

Only in this context can the crucial nature of the breaking of divine being into history be understood. The breakthrough occurs in the soul of Abraham, the one who had died to the fated, unfree, cosmogonic world with its cycles of eternal return. The divine Revelation and the order given by God—in both a cosmic creation and in the created order of the individual soul in its fragile existence in freedom under God—are established in a covenant. In Abraham and in Israel, the meaning of human existence is not governed or ordered by cosmogonic cycles, nor by the cultures that form them; it comes from the transcendent God who is present in history.

The covenant in its fullness is what constitutes the bond in both its outer and inner symbols. The inner symbols of love and fidelity form and strengthen Israel. The outer symbols mean that what Israel is given in Revelation is a truth, not just for herself, but for all the nations of the world.

In the Patriarchs, Moses and the Exodus, and the Decalogue, the ups and downs of fidelity to the covenant (berith) convey the sacred existence of Israel as a call to order her gifts and freedom to worship and holiness. Not surprisingly, therefore, when the bishops of the Second Vatican Council spoke about the uniqueness of Judaism in Nostra Aetate, they noted that, when the Church "searches into the mystery" of its own existence, "it remembers the bond that spiritually ties the people of the New Covenant to Abraham's stock" (NA, no. 4).

The Church cannot grasp the mystery of her own existence and constitution by the Lord without constantly re-appropriating, and more deeply entering into, God's break with cosmogonic ignorance and deformation of the human soul and self, and his gift of freedom and promise; the Church cannot do so without the people of the berith. Indeed, the Church cannot forget what she has received in God's Revelation "through the people with whom God in His inexpressible mercy deigned to establish the Ancient Covenant" (NA, no. 4). And while it is true that "the Jewish authorities and those who followed their lead pressed for the death of Christ" (see Jn 19:6) nonetheless, what happened in his Passion cannot be "blamed upon all the Jews then living, nor upon the Jews of today" (NA, no. 4).

Therefore the Church deplores the hatred, persecution, and displays of antisemitism directed against the Jews at any time and from any source. "As the Church has always held and holds now, Christ underwent His passion and death freely, because of the sins of men and out of infinite love, in order that all may reach salvation" (NA, no. 4) (see Lk 6:16).

The Church's Self-Understanding

The Church comes to self-understanding and knowledge of her existence and purpose through the mystery of the life, death, and Resurrection of Jesus Christ. He calls and teaches his Apostles the truth of God's purpose of salvation from sin, evil, and death. This is done by the deeds and teachings of Christ that identify him as the One sent by the Father. His mission is to open to all those who have been created, and who are called to share and participate in the intimacy and delight of the life of God.

The Incarnation of the Word in Jesus Christ reveals the absolutely supernatural and definitive redemption of the human race, not by removing evil and sin through power, but by transforming evil into good through the life, death, and Resurrection of Jesus. The Spirit too is sent in mission, "flooding our hearts" and inwardly drawing persons into friendship with God the Father through incorporation into the life of Christ. The mission of truth and love enters into temporality through the outer words and deeds of Jesus, which live on in the community through the inner mission of the Spirit and through the outer expression in the Church, Scripture, and sacraments, and which can only be recognized as true in the light and through the gift of faith.

The mediation of the missions and their engagement with all of human history is not handed on by the establishment of a school, but by the call of Christ to the Apostles with the teaching: "Go, therefore, and make disciples of all nations, baptizing them in the name of the Father, and of the Son, and of the holy Spirit, teaching them to observe all that I have commanded you. And behold, I am with you always, until the end of the age" (Mt 28:19-20).

The command to evangelize is given first to the Apostles, and through them to those who have been given the gift of faith and a share in the promise of salvation. To follow Christ is first and foremost to allow the inner Word of the Lord to dwell in one's own soul. It is the same Lord who suffers and dies for the salvation of all; from such dwelling in holiness, the outer word of the Apostles seeks to be in conformity with the inner Word, so that their lives become manifestations of the light of truth and self-sacrificing love.

The whole of the Church is called to enter into imitating Christ's life, sharing in the sacramental unity that binds believers to the Risen One and to each other. All are called to evangelize within their specific vocations and status of life. Not surprisingly, just as the natural cosmogonic peoples created societies and cultures that sought to replicate the eternal cycles of the universe, so Christians are called to translate the mission of truth and charity into every nook and cranny of their daily life, both in its personal and private dimensions, and in the institutions of social and cultural order in which they live. When a culture in a Christian context becomes a series of institutional deformations, evangelization is both absent and needed.

It must be noted that evangelization is not proselytization. The *Dogmatic Constitution on the Church* (*Lumen Gentium*) reminds us that the mystery of redemption is given and affected through suffering and humility; it is not given through power that would overwhelm the inner word of truth and love as potentially present in each person that God creates. Therefore, authentic evangelization moves deliberately but humbly, for Christians may turn the cardinal mission given to them, the Church, and the Apostles into "a forced conversion," one that does not engage the mystery of light in truth and charity but that occurs for lesser and corrupted reasons.

While evangelization and proselytization have been conflated in popular parlance as being the same thing, it is important to note that, in the New Testament, the terms are carefully differentiated; a proselyte refers to a person who converts to the Jewish religion. (Mt 23:15; Acts 2:11; 6:5, etc.)

Because proselytization was at times how the essential evangelical character of Catholic life confronted Jewish people, today we know the concerns, indeed anger and fear, that Jews have about evangelization. Evangelization, on the other hand, is an essential character of faith, going back to the Revelation of God and the Trinitarian mission in the New Testament. The deep discomfort of the Jews requires us to listen carefully to Jewish voices about their covenant, religious life, and sense of the Christian community. As Pope John Paul II noted in an audience with representatives of Jewish organizations on March 12, 1979,

> In virtue of her divine mission, and her very nature, the church must preach Jesus Christ to the world (*Ad Gentes*, no. 2). Lest the witness of Catholics to Jesus Christ should give offense to Jews, they must take care to live and spread their Christian faith while maintaining the strictest respect for religious liberty in line with the teaching of the Second Vatican Council (*Dignitatis Humanae*). They will likewise strive to understand the difficulties which arise for the Jewish soul—rightly imbued with an extremely high, pure notion of the divine transcendence—

when faced with the mystery of the Incarnate Word (Guidelines, no. 1).[9]

It may be helpful here to bring some attention to the enormous internal difficulties of the bishops at the Second Vatican Council during the development of the decree *On the Mission Activity of the Church* (*Ad Gentes*) (AG).[10] The disagreements in theological, historical, and cultural areas were deep and often trying for the participants during the formulation of the various schemata of this decree. Conflicts existed over the foundational principles of missions and their relationship to colonial nations, over the sending of missionaries to emerging nations, over the slow but growing number of native bishops and clergy, and over the oversight of the "foreign missions" by the *Propaganda Fide*.[11] At the 116th general congregation of the Council on November 6, 1964, Paul VI took part at the opening of the reflection on the decree. Speaking of its importance, he noted that the salvation of the world depends on the fulfillment of the missionary command. He praised developments in the schema and noted that new ways must be found.

Indeed, Paul VI would suggest such ways and means in his encyclical letter of August 6, 1964, *On the Church* (*Ecclesiam Suam*) (ES), in which he spoke of a relationship of dialogue as "a dialogue of salvation" and evangelization. This, in turn, opened further issues of great importance that were part of the decree and led to further clarification of issues that had arisen in the Council. In the encyclical, the pope spoke of dialogue with the world as "a recognized method of the apostolate. It is a way of making spiritual contact"(ES, no. 81)."[12] He further noted a fourfold manner in which the Church's "dialogue of salvation" engages with the whole of the world. These four ways are (1) the dialogue with the whole of mankind; (2) the dialogue with the followers of other religions; (3) the dialogue with other Christians; and (4) the inner dialogue of the Church herself.[13]

Perhaps the most succinct account of the relationship of dialogue to the person of Christ and to the life of evangelization is found in *On the Mission Activity of the Church* (*Ad Gentes*) (AG), where the Council insisted that the followers of Christ who are

> profoundly pervaded by the Spirit of Christ, should know and converse with those among whom they live. . . . Through sincere and patient dialogue they themselves might learn of the riches which a generous God has distributed among the nations. They must at the same time endeavor to illuminate these riches with

the light of the Gospel, set them free, and bring them once more under the dominion of God the savior. (AG, no. 11)

Evangelization, when joined with dialogue, includes the task of teaching what Christ has taught through his mission of truth and learning from those who also live in the Spirit's presence. This means that evangelization includes more than teaching and preaching; it includes developing ways to offer a common witness to that which is the substance of what is human, as has been shown, or implied, by the missions of Son and Spirit.

Within the Synod on Evangelization in 1974, the bishops' discussion continued trying to relate the program for dialogue with that of evangelization. At that synod, the plan for a final document was never completed, but the schema that was proposed noted that "Interreligious dialogue must not be considered extrinsic to the Church's mission of evangelization. . . . In itself it is already a concrete expression of the Church's mission."[14] Particular attention was given to the mission of the Holy Spirit, but it was unclear how that mission related to the mission of the Son.

Paul VI's apostolic exhortation of December 8, 1975, *On Evangelization in the Modern World* (*Evangelii Nuntiandi*) (EN), showed a deep concern that the right balance and proper tension of relating dialogue and evangelization had not yet been realized. In the exhortation it is clear that the mission of the Word of truth could not be displaced, as it were, by that of the Holy Spirit alone. But the document also speaks of the expansion of the meaning of evangelization to many levels, so that it includes not only preaching of Christ, but also developing an "explicit message, adapted to the different situations constantly being realized."[15]

Listening to Jewish Concerns

Given the importance of dialogue and evangelization in the Church's mission, let us consider some remarks by one of the great religious thinkers of Judaism as he reflects about Jewish existence in the initial covenant that God does not abrogate. I wish that we had time to listen to, or to read, numerous pages of the modern Jewish theologian and mystic Abraham Heschel; but while we do not have such time, that we engage and enter into his insights and mediations. I could not more deeply encourage.

In the following passages, Heschel speaks of the need for Christians and Jews to live according to the mystery of God's presence and of God's

Word and command, and to do so with a recovery of reverence and of respect, while holding together what binds us and what separates us.

Is Judaism, is Christianity, ready to face the challenge? When I speak about the radiance of the Bible in the minds of man, I do not mean its being a theme for Information, Please but rather an openness to God's presence in the Bible, the continuous ongoing effort for a breakthrough in the soul of man, the guarding of the precarious position of being human, even a little higher than human, despite defiance and in the face of despair.[16]

Our era marks the end of complacency, the end of evasion, the end of self-reliance. Jews and Christians share the perils and the fears; we stand on the brink of the abyss together. (Heschel, p. 237)

We are all involved with one another. Spiritual betrayal on the part of one of us affects the faith of all of us. Views adopted in one community have an impact on other communities. Today religious isolationism is a myth. For all the profound differences in perspective and substance, Judaism is sooner or later affected by the intellectual, moral, and spiritual events within the Christian society, and vice versa. (237)

We fail to realize that while different exponents of faith in the world of religion continue to be wary of the ecumenical movement, there is another ecumenical movement, worldwide in extent and influence: nihilism. We must choose between interfaith and internihilism. Cynicism is not parochial. Should religions insist upon the illusion of complete isolation? Should we refuse to be on speaking terms with one another and hope for each other's failure? Or should we pray for each other's health and help one another in preserving one's respective legacy, in preserving a common legacy? (237)

The great spiritual renewal within the Roman Catholic Church, inspired by Pope John XXIII, is a manifestation of the dimension of depth of religious existence. It already has opened many hearts and unlocked many precious insights. There is a longing for peace in the hearts of man. But peace is not the same as the absence of war. Peace among men depends upon a relationship of reverence for each other. (288)

A religious man is a person who holds God and man in one thought at one time, at all times, who suffers in himself harm done to others, whose greatest passion is compassion, whose greatest strength is love and defiance of despair. (289)

The primary aim of these reflections is to inquire how a Jew out of his commitment and a Christian out of his commitment can find a religious basis for communication and cooperation on matters relevant to their moral and spiritual concern in spite of disagreement. (289)

I suggest that the most significant basis for meeting of men of different religious traditions is the level of fear and trembling, of humility and contrition, where our individual moments of faith are mere waves in the endless ocean of mankind's reaching out for God, where all formulations and articulations appear as understatements, where our souls are swept away by the awareness of the urgency of answering God's commandment, while stripped of pretension and conceit we sense the tragic insufficiency of human faith. (239-240)

Both communication and separation are necessary. We must preserve our individuality as well as foster care for one another, reverence, understanding, cooperation. (243)

Heschel calls Christians to engage with Jews in living in the presence of God in the face of the modern age's doubt, in fostering human dignity and reverence in a common witness of what it means to live in God's life, and to acknowledge together a common need for holiness, for humility, for repentance, and for dialogue together.

On the matter of dialogue and its profound implications, it is important to remember the model of dialogue that was established between Eugen Rosenstock-Huessy and Franz Rosenzweig. From Rosenstock-Huessy's critical analysis of the importance of language and the nature of dialogue and conversation and its implications for Catholicism in the modern world, to his establishment of the famous Patmos Circle of 1915-1923, to his engagement with the Jewish scholar Rosenzweig that began in 1913, we see what it means to be true to religious faiths, and to be able to challenge one another to the deepest core of one's life so as to mediate, in dialogue, religious mystery through the mystery of language. This activity opened up, for both of them, the common challenge of living according to Revelation, and of doing so in complementarity with one another, with each being opened into intimacy with God.[17]

In this bond, Rosenstock-Huessy speaks of the form of our religious responsibility that we have in dialogue, a responsibility that awakens in us dimensions that we alone cannot recognize. He especially knows this about the conversations with persons of the Jewish religion, in which we must listen to the mystery that is borne in their being. He is clear about the consequences of this: "I respond although I will be changed."[18]

We, of course, can only resonate deeply with such requests for honest collaboration. The tasks that will flow from such effort and grace will take time to flourish. As Cardinal Walter Kasper remarked at a lecture given at Boston College in November 2001, "We are at the beginning of the beginning."[19]

Jewish Relations and Christian Evangelization

Having considered the reflections of Hershel and the writings of Paul VI, we come to reflect on the consequences of what constitutes the Church, what constitutes dialogue, what shapes the levels of evangelization for common witness discovered through dialogue, and what constitutes the Jewish people in the covenant with Abraham as uniquely bound to Christians, and specifically, to the Catholic understanding of evangelization. John Paul II, in *Redeemer of Man* (*Redemptor Hominis*) (RH) immediately returns to the effort of his predecessor in identifying what the patristic writers had acknowledged: the importance of natural religion as pointing to one truth and to one single goal to which is "directed the deepest aspiration of the human spirit as expressed in its quest for God and also in its quest, through its tending towards God, for the full dimension of its humanity, or in other words for the full meaning of human life. The Council gave particular attention to the Jewish religion, recalling the great spiritual heritage common to Christians and Jews" (RH, no. 11).[20]

It is essential, therefore, to develop religious, spiritual, and theological dialogue with the Jewish community. In this dialogue, we are committed to learning and participating in the mission of the Word/Logos so that we make manifest the mystery of the self-sacrificing love of God that is given to us only by going through the covenant with Abraham. Thus, the bond of Jewish relations and Catholic evangelization invites us into a profound sense and study of the mystery of the Church in her relationship with the Jewish religion. The insight that the importance of dialogue brings to the responsibility of evangelization begins in respect and reverence for those who are God's first people.[21]

John Paul II has reminded us about the special importance of the way in which relations with Jews—especially as we come to know the mystery of God's work in the Jewish people—leads us to confront situations that are antisemitic, for such acts "must be held to be sinful."[22] The first element of our presence with Judaism is to properly assess antisemitic actions or words and announce a clear rejection of the purpose to injure, to vilify, and to hate.

Second, we need a dialogue of life in which we identify common issues of human concern, such as those related to the meaning of family and work, education and economics, and political and cultural possibilities and dangers. We must attend to times in which we share the joys and sorrows of human life, take opportunities to rejoice with members of local Jewish communities in their achievements, and invite them to share in our own.

Third, we must collaborate with Jewish persons—and, if possible, institutions—on issues that relate to human rights and are grounded in natural law and biblical witness. Fourth, we need to develop religious conversations among our peoples and prepare Catholics to enter into conversation with religious Jewish people, so as to experience and learn how the mystery of God informs and guides both their lives and ours—together, yet differently. This can be especially helpful in commonly drawing us into the eschatological sense of God's work in our midst through his Spirit.

Fifth, we can promote theological dialogues with persons who are trained in the intellectual dimensions of the Catholic and Jewish traditions so as to further understand the bonds and the tensions that together shape our relations in the mystery of salvation.[23]

Through our evangelization with Jewish people, we become like Christ, in the same way he was to the people with whom he lived and whose lives he shared in their joy and sorrow. We must witness to the fullness of his abiding love for his people, from the mystery of his humanity in Israel and his divinity, to his self-sacrifice for the life of his Church and the world. Religious Jewish people have an enormous importance for Catholics by their requiring fidelity of us to our faith and conversion of our hearts and minds to God.

From within such conversion and holiness in our own Church, we also teach what Christ has handed to us in Revelation: for us, Jesus is not only Jewish in his humanity, his life of prayer, and his culture, but he is also God, the Son of the Father, the Messiah that brings salvation for the world. Because we accept his divinity as enfleshed in the whole of the Jewish tradition, we pray Jewish Psalms and prayers; our liturgy is grounded in Jewish worship, our quest for holiness is related to the moral teachings of the Hebrew Scriptures, and much of our learning comes from the Jewish prophets.[24]

It is no wonder then that in the *Declaration on the Relation of the Church to Non-Christian Religions* (*Nostra Aetate*) the bishops note that when the Council "searches into the mystery of the Church, it remembers the bond that spiritually ties the people of the New Covenant to Abraham's stock" (NA, no. 4)

This recalls also the importance of what Heschel notes regarding the acknowledgement of our separateness as well as our need for communication. Because of this separateness, we are called to be faithful to the Church's life and the constant commission of the Scripture. We know that Israel is called to fidelity, as is the Church. We know that proselytization is unacceptable and disrespectful of the mystery of Jewish life and presence.

During his pastoral visit to France in October 1988, John Paul II met with the Jewish community in Strasbourg. In his talk, he spoke of the tension that contributes to the relationship of Jews and Catholics.

> It is through your prayer, your history and your experience of faith that you continue to affirm the fundamental unity of God, his fatherhood and mercy towards every man and woman, the mystery of his plan of salvation, and the consequences that come from it according to the principles expressed by the Prophets, in the commitment for justice, peace and other ethical values. With the greatest respect for the Jewish religious identity, I would also like to emphasize for us Christians, the Church, the people of God and Mystical body of Christ, is called throughout her journey to proclaim to all the Good News of salvation in the consolation of the Holy Spirit.[25]

As officers of evangelization and ecumenism, we experience this tension within the Church, and for the Jewish community, this tension is at the heart of the mystery that both joins and separates us, until God will bring his plan of salvation into the full light of his glory.

Fr. Arthur L. Kennedy

Fr. Kennedy graduated from St. John's Seminary College in Brighton, Massachusetts, and was ordained to the priesthood in 1966 for the Archdiocese of Boston. He studied at the Pontifical Gregorian University in Rome, where he earned an STL in theology in 1967. In 1978, he obtained a doctorate in systematic theology/philosophy of religion from Boston University. For twenty-eight years, he was a professor of theology at the University of St. Thomas, Minnesota. He has been a member of the board of directors of the Jay Philips Center for Jewish Christian Learning in St. Paul, Minnesota since 1991. In 2002, Fr. Kennedy was appointed executive director of the Secretariat for Ecumenical and Interreligious Affairs at the United States Conference of Catholic Bishops in Washington, D.C.

NOTES

1   Paul VI, *Declaration on the Relation of the Church to Non-Christian Religions* (*Nostra Aetate*) (Vatican City: Libreria Editrice Vaticana, October 28, 1965).

2   See Cicero, *De Natura Deorum*, II xxviii, for relegere; Lactantius, *Divinae Institutiones*, IV, xxviii, for *religare*; St. Augustine, *De Civitate Dei*, X, iii, for *religere*; St. Augustine, *Retractiones* I, xiii, for his shift to *religare*; and St. Thomas Aquinas, *Summa Theologica*, II-II, Q. lxxxi, a. 1, for all three definitions. Aquinas finds an intelligibility in religion that leads him to specify it as a virtue connected with justice in relationship to God and then to differentiate its various aspects (II-II, Q. 81-100). For an analysis of the relationship of Cicero's reflection on religion and society, see Eric Voegelin, *The New Science of Politics* (Chicago: University of Chicago Press, 1957), 89-91. In a number of places Bernard Lonergan, SJ, speaks of religion as grounded in the dynamic spirit of self-transcendence. He finds its increasing perfection in the flow of consciousness from below, up, and in the gift of God's love in the vector from above down. See chapter four on religion in Bernard Lonergan, *Method in Theology* (New York: Herder and Herder, 1972),101-124. For more on the relation of metaphysics, mystery, and knowledge of God, see Lonergan, *Insight: A Study of Human Understanding* (London: Longmans, Green and Co., 1958), 634-730.

3   For an account of the relationship of God and culture, see Christopher Dawson, *The Age of the Gods: A Study in the Origins of Culture in Pre-historic Europe and the Ancient East* (London: J. Murray, 1928). For a critical and appreciative analysis of the Babylonian version of cosmogonic religion and the translation of its meaning and consequences into society see chapter six in Dawson, "The City State and the Development of the Sumerian Culture." For a helpful account of the developments of the human and social sciences as necessary for the development of cultural knowledge and research, see Dawson, *Progress and Religion: An Historical Enquiry into the Causes and Development of Progress and its Relationship to Religion* (London: Sheed and Ward, 1929).

4   See Beryl Smalley, *The Study of the Bible in the Middle Ages* (Notre Dame, IN: University of Notre Dame Press, 1978).

5   See Aaron Milavec, *The* Didache: *Faith, Hope and Life of the Earliest Christian Community, 50-75 C.E.* (Mahwah, NJ: Newman Press, 2003). This is an excellent critical edition and commentary on the *Didache* and its Jewish sources.

6   See Eric Voegelin, *Order and History, Volume I: Israel and Revelation* (Columbia, MO: University of Missouri Press, 1999), 81-84 and 91-150.

7   St. Thomas Aquinas, *Summa Theologica*, trans. Fathers of the English Dominican Province (New York: Benziger Bros., 1947). Also see Matthew Levering, *Christ as Fulfillment of Torah and Law: A Study on Thomas Aquinas* (Notre Dame, IN: Notre Dame University Press, 2000).

8   Paul VI, *Dogmatic Constitution on the Church* (*Lumen Gentium*) (Vatican City: Libreria Editrice Vaticana, November 21, 1964).

9   John Paul II, *Addresses and Homilies on Ecumenism 1978-1980*, ed. John B. Sheerin CSP and John F. Hotchkin (Washington, DC: USCCB, 1981). 20. Also see Second Vatican Council, *On the Mission Activity of the Church* (*Ad Gentes Divinitus*) (Vatican City: Libreria Editrice Vaticana, December 7, 1965), and Second Vatican Council, *Declaration on Religious Liberty* (*Dignitatis Humanae*) (Vatican City: Libreria Editrice Vaticana, December 7, 1965), and Vatican Commission for Religious Relations with the Jews, *Guidelines and Suggestions for Jewish-Christian Relations* (Vatican City, Libreria Editrice Vaticana, December 1, 1974).

10 Second Vatican Council, *On the Mission Activity of the Church* (*Ad Gentes Divinitus*) (Vatican City: Libreria Editrice Vaticana, December 7, 1965).

11 John Paul II, *On the Permanent Validity of the Church's Missionary Mandate* (*Redemptoris Missio*) (Vatican City: Libreria Editrice Vaticana, December 7, 1990), nos. 52-54. Also see Philip Jenkins, *The Next Christendom: The Coming of Global Christianity* (Oxford

and New York: Oxford University Press, 2002), 56-57. Jenkins speaks of the success of the original missions with their colonial connections, which were in time transformed, while the faith continued to flourish and grow as a result of both the original foreign missions and the native bishops, clergy, and laity.

12 Paul VI, *On the Church* (*Ecclesiam Suam*) (Vatican City: Libreria Editrice Vaticana, August 6, 1964).

13 See Second Vatican *Council, Constitution on the Church in the Modern World* (*Gaudium et Spes*) (Washington, DC: USCCB, 1996), no. 92, where the fourfold spheres of dialogue are reordered.

14 Jacques Dupuis, SJ, "Interreligious Dialogue in the Church's Evangelizing Mission: Twenty Years of Evolution of a Theological Concept," in René Latourelle, *Vatican II: Assessment and Perspectives* 3 (Mahwah, NJ: Paulist Press, 1989): 248.

15 Paul VI, *On Evangelization in the Modern World* (*Evangelii Nuntiandi*) (Washington, DC: USCCB, 1997), no. 29.

16 Abraham Joshua Heschel, *Moral Grandeur and Spiritual Audacity*, ed. Susannah Heschel (New York: Noonday Press, 1997), 236. All subsequent passages noted above are taken from this collection of Heschel's essays.

17 For a careful analysis of the bond between Rosenstock-Huessy and Rosenzweig, see Harold Stahmer, *Speak That I May See: The Religious Significance of Language* (New York: Macmillan Company, 1968). Stahmer identifies other relations between Jews and Catholics and other Christians that were underway, starting from the 1920s.

18 Harold Stahmer, Speak *That I May See: The Religious Significance of Language* (New York: Macmillan Company, 1968), 112-113. As Stahmer indicates, Rosenstack-Huessy uses this phrase as a motto to underline the social nature of truth and its "costly commitment for each individual."

19 Cardinal Walter Kasper, *The Commission for Religious Relations with the Jews: A Crucial Endeavor of the Catholic Church* (Speech at Boston College: November 6, 2002). Cardinal Kasper indicated that we are in a very early stage in Jewish-Catholic dialogue in his presentation.

20 John Paul II, *Redeemer of Man* (*Redemptoris Hominis*) (Vatican City: Libreria Editrice Vaticana, March 4, 1979).

21 For an example of John Paul II's profound appropriation of Revelation in the Hebrew Scripture and Jewish religion, see *On the Mercy of God* (*Dives in Misericordia*) (Vatican City: Libreria Editrice Vaticana, November 30, 1980), no. 4.

22 Eugene Fisher and Leon Klenicki, ed., *Pope John Paul II: Spiritual Pilgrimage: Texts on Jews and Judaism, 1979-1995* (New York: Crossroad Press, 1996),.82.

23 Pontifical Council for Interreligious Dialogue, *Dialogue and Proclamation: Reflection and Orientations on Interreligious Dialogue and the Proclamation of the Gospel of Jesus Christ* (Vatican City: Libreria Editrice Vaticana, May 19, 1991), no. 42. The four modes of dialogue as suggested by the document are modified here for application to the unique relationship of Catholics and Jews.

24 See Joseph Fitzmyer, SJ, *Essays on the Semitic Background of the New Testament* (Missoula, MT: Scholars Press, 1971). The Scriptural interstices are shown as mediated by the Qur'an literature.

25 Fisher and Klenicki, 126.

INTERRELIGIOUS IMPLICATIONS FOR CATHOLIC EVANGELIZATION

Fr. Thomas Ryan, CSP

I f one were to ask the normal Catholic church attendee what "evangelization" means, the response would likely be along the lines of "announcing the person and teachings of Jesus Christ to those who have not yet heard or accepted them." Rare would be the church member, I would hazard to say, who would appreciate that the formal "church word" for this is "proclamation," and that in recent Catholic teaching, "evangelization" has been much more broadly defined.

In his apostolic exhortation *On Evangelization in the Modern World* (*Evangelii Nuntiandi*) (EN), Pope Paul VI declares, "For the Church, evangelizing means bringing the Good News into all the strata of humanity, and through its influence transforming humanity from within and making it new."[1]

In his encyclical on missionary activity, *On the Permanent Validity of the Church's Missionary Mandate* (hereafter *Redemptoris Missio*) (RM), Pope John Paul II, built on this broad concept of evangelization and distinguished three spheres. The first relates to "the mission to the Gentiles" and is directed to peoples who do not yet believe in Christ. The second sphere, re-evangelization, is aimed at rekindling Christian faith in regions where the Gospel has taken root but where the people have lost a living sense of the faith, so that they need to be converted to Christ once more. The third sphere, pastoral care, is the deeper insertion of the Gospel in the hearts and minds of faithful Christians, so that they will be able to think, feel, speak, and act in full accordance with the mind of Christ.[2] Such pastoral care falls within the comprehensive idea of evangelization set forth by Paul VI.

The United States Conference of Catholic Bishops' *National Plan and Strategy for Catholic Evangelization in the United States, Go and Make Disciples* (GMD), addresses the questions of why we evangelize, how evangelization happens, and what the goals of evangelization are.[3] I will look at the implications of interreligious dialogue for Catholic evangelization through the prism of these three questions, and when it comes to the third, the goal, I will focus in particular on the goal of that element of the Church's evangelizing mission that is interreligious dialogue.

Why We Evangelize

Go and Make Disciples cites several reasons: "We must evangelize because the Lord Jesus commanded us to (no. 28). . . We evangelize because people must be brought to the salvation that Jesus the Lord offers in and through the Church (no. 30) . . . because we have experienced the love of Christ, we want to share it"(no. 33). Once we have said this, we must immediately add that evangelization in Catholic understanding and practice is a multi-layered and complex reality. It encompasses proclamation of what God has done in Christ for our salvation, but it is never simply proclamation.

When other Christian churches speak about evangelism, by and large they mean the direct preaching of Jesus Christ. When, for example, the World Council of Churches established its Commission on World Mission and Evangelism, "mission" included activities like healthcare, economic development, and education, while evangelism more pointedly referred to converting people to Christ.

In Catholic usage, however, the evangelizing mission of the Church encompasses all these things. Thus Paul VI declared that proclamation "occupies such an important place in evangelization that it has often become synonymous with it; and yet it is only one aspect of evangelization"(EN, 22)

In 1964 Paul VI wrote in On the Church—generally considered the Magna Carta of dialogue in its various forms—that the Church must be a people in dialogue with the world.4 But he did not take a position on the exact place that interreligious dialogue might occupy in the Church's mission. Evangelii Nuntiandi, written eleven years later, does not even mention dialogue. The Second Vatican Council encouraged dialogue with other religions, but it did not declare it to be part of the Church's evangelizing mission. This development has come about only in three subsequent documents: Dialogue and Mission (1984), Redemptoris Missio (1990), and Dialogue and Proclamation (1991).[5]

The first of these three is notable in several respects and merits our immediate attention. In 1984 the Holy See produced the document The Attitude of the Church toward the Followers of Other Religions: Reflections and Orientations on Dialogue and Mission (hereafter Dialogue and

Mission). This document addressed what had been an abiding concern since the 1960s: the relationship between mission and interreligious dialogue. In the 1984 document, we find a shift, quietly made but momentous in its implications, that marked an evolution beyond the teaching of Paul VI and the Council. Interreligious dialogue was no longer described as distinct from but related to the evangelizing mission of the Church. It now was viewed, in other words, as a constitutive element of the Church's evangelizing mission.

The members of the Vatican's then-Secretariat for Non-Christians came to this conclusion themselves and included it in their draft of *Dialogue and Mission*. When John Paul II spoke to them at the plenary session on March 3, 1984, at which time the draft was presented for discussion, he reflected on this theme, saying that dialogue is fundamental for the Church, based on the very life of the triune God, as well as on respect and love for every human person:

> As far as the local churches are concerned, they must commit themselves in this direction, helping all the faithful to respect and to esteem the values, traditions and convictions of other believers. At the same time they must promote a solid and suitable religious education of the Christians themselves so that they know how to give convinced witness to the great gift of faith. No local church is exempt from this duty, which is made urgent. . . migration, travel, social communications and personal choices.[6]

The pope affirmed this dynamic tension between dialogue and proclamation toward the end of his remarks, saying:

> Authentic dialogue becomes witness, and true evangelization is accomplished by respecting and listening to one another. Even though 'there is a time for everything' (Eccles. 3:1-8), prudence and discernment will teach us what is appropriate in each particular situation: collaboration, witness, listening, or exchange of values. Saints like Francis of Assisi and great missionaries like Matteo Ricci and Charles de Foucauld are examples of this.[7]

The formal issuance of the document *Dialogue and Mission* is dated two months after the 1984 plenary session. It describes "mission" as a "single but complex and articulated reality" with several components:

> Mission is already constituted by the simple presence and witness of the Christian life. . . . the service of humankind and all forms of activity for social development and for the struggle against poverty and the

structures that produce it. Also, there is liturgical life and that of prayer and contemplation. . . . There is also the dialogue in which Christians meet the followers of other religions in order to walk together toward truth and to work together in projects of common concern. Finally, there is announcement and catechesis in which the good news of the Gospel is proclaimed and its consequences for life and culture are analyzed.[8]

The evangelizing mission of the Church is indeed a complex reality, and the above listing of elements in Catholic evangelization could be further expanded to include intraChristian relations as well as dialogue with those who profess no faith at all. But *Dialogue and Mission* gives us plenty to work with for our present purposes of looking at the interreligious implications for Catholic evangelization. These elements provide a convenient description of how evangelization happens.

The Simple Presence and Witness of the Christian Life

The following words, popularly attributed to St. Francis of Assisi, say it well: "Preach the gospel wherever you go. If necessary, use words." We are the only Gospel that some people will ever read. The "book" of our behavior toward others and God's creation is always open for others to see. Perhaps I can best illustrate my meaning here with some reverse examples, for this kind of evangelization is a reciprocal reality.

My own practice of the faith has been challenged and deepened by the simple presence and witness of members of other living faiths. In watching Buddhist monks make their three prostrations before a statue of the Buddha with such devotion and mindfulness each time they enter and leave the temple, I have asked myself, "With what reverence and attentiveness do I genuflect before the Blessed Sacrament and celebrate Mass?" In witnessing Orthodox Jews heading for their synagogue on the Sabbath and afterwards enjoying the parks with their families, I am called to look at my own practice of keeping the day of the Lord's Resurrection free each week just for praying and playing and nurturing relationships. In witnessing the fasting of Muslims during Ramadan, I am moved to examine whether the middle leg of that traditional tripod of prayer, fasting, and works of charity is listing or carrying its weight in my own life. We should never minimize or underestimate the evangelizing potential of the simple witness of living our faith.

The Service of Humankind and All Forms of Activity for Social Development

I spent a month in 1991 with Benedictine Fr. Bede Griffiths at his Christian *ashram*, Shantivanam (Forest of Peace), in South India. Fr. Bede, who died in 1993, was one of the great pioneers of interreligious dialogue in India. One day we were talking about the local Hindu-Christian dialogue between members of the ashram and people in the village nearby. Fr. Bede said that when, after the first few sessions, he had invited the Hindu members of the dialogue to come and join them for meditation at Shantivanam, they reacted with surprise. "What? Do you mean you Christians meditate?" they exclaimed. "We thought you just ran schools and orphanages and hospitals!"

The Christian record on social action is well known and is in its own right a powerful source of inspiration for members of other living faiths. Buddhists and the Dalai Lama, for example, are quick to recognize that they have been challenged by and have learned from Christian activism for justice and peace. In its own way, Buddhist social activism is now advancing God's reign of justice and peace in the world in new ways.

Liturgical Life, Prayer, and Contemplation

There is no better story to demonstrate the evangelizing potential of good liturgy than the one told about the pagan Grand Prince Vladimir of Kiev in the late tenth century. He reportedly sent envoys to different parts of the world to examine the local religions and to advise him of which would be best for his kingdom. When the envoys returned, they recommended the faith of the Byzantine Greek Christians. The envoys related that when they attended the divine liturgy in the cathedral of Hagia Sophia in Constantinople, "we did not know if we were in heaven or on earth." After the Baptism of Prince Vladimir, many of his followers were baptized in the waters of the Dnieper River in 988. Thus, thanks to good liturgy, Byzantine Christianity became the faith of the three peoples who trace their origins to Rus' of Kiev: the Ukrainians, Belarusians, and Russians.[9]

We could all tell a story or two from our own experience of parishes that draw people from all over town because of the quality of their worship or preaching. But sometimes it is simply the commitment to personal prayer, or the atmosphere of faith in the home, or the silent witness to the divine transcendent of the monastery on the hill that becomes an instrument of grace for someone.

Edith Stein—or Sr. Benedetta of the Cross, as she came to be known after her conversion and entry into a Carmelite community—is considered a good candidate to become one of the few women given the title of "Doctor of the Church." Edith was raised as an Orthodox Jew, and her book Life in a Jewish Family, written to counter the increasingly antisemitic climate of Germany in the 1930s, shows her abiding love and respect for the tradition in which she was raised. But before her conversion, and in relation to her experience at the university, she had been a committed atheist for several years. What brought her back to faith in God was the way in which the devout Catholic family of a friend dealt with the loss of a loved one.

We never know what is going on in the hearts and minds of those present at wakes and funerals, weddings and Baptisms. But undoubtedly more hearts are touched and lives changed than just those of the faithful when they celebrate their rites and kneel in prayer.

Dialogue in Which Christians Meet the Followers of Other Religions

Dialogue and Mission makes clear that dialogue is not just a matter of theological discussion. It outlines several forms of dialogue:

> *The dialogue of life*: Dialogue is a manner of acting, an attitude; a spirit which guides one's conduct. It implies concern, respect, and hospitality toward the other. Every follower of Christ is called to bring the Gospel into any environment in which he or she lives and works: familial, social, educational, artistic, economic, or political. Dialogue thus finds its place in the dynamism of the Church's mission.

> *The dialogue of works or action*: Collaboration with others for goals of a humanitarian, social, economic or political nature which are directed towards the liberation and advancement of humankind. This kind of dialogue often occurs where Christians and followers of other religions confront together the problems of the world.

> *The dialogue of theological exchange*: Specialists seek to deepen the understanding of their respective religious heritages and the appreciation of each other's spiritual values, always bearing in

mind the need to search for the ultimate truth. They may also wish to apply something of their expertise to the problems which must be faced by humanity.

The dialogue of religious experience: Persons rooted in their own religious traditions can share their experiences of prayer, contemplation, faith, and duty, as well as their expressions and ways of searching for the absolute. This type of dialogue can be a mutual enrichment and fruitful cooperation for promoting and preserving the highest values and spiritual ideals. (DM, nos. 835-842)

Over the last several years, the Pontifical Council for Interreligious Dialogue has been exploring the spiritual dimensions of interreligious dialogue. Two plenaries on the topic have been held on and a text has been prepared on *The Spirituality of Interreligious Dialogue*, which will be forthcoming in the not-too-distant future.

Announcement and Catechesis in Which the Good News Is Proclaimed

Full evangelization must always be directly connected to the Lord Jesus Christ. "There is no true evangelization if the name, the teaching, the life, the promises, the kingdom and the mystery of Jesus of Nazareth, the Son of God are not proclaimed," wrote Paul VI (EN, no. 22).

Proclamation happens when the word of Jesus speaks to people's hearts and minds as "Good News." *Go and Make Disciples* distills the essence of that Gospel in these words:

Our message of faith proclaims an eternally faithful God, creating all in love and sustaining all with gracious care. We proclaim that God, whose love is unconditional, offers us divine life even in the face of our sins, failures, and inadequacies. We believe in a God who became one of us in Jesus, God's Son, whose death and resurrection bring us salvation. We believe that the risen Christ sends his own Spirit upon us when we respond to him in faith and repentance, making us his people, the Church, and giving us the power of new life and guiding us to our eternal destiny. (GMD, no. 20)

The Pontifical Council for Interreligious Dialogue's text *Dialogue and Proclamation* (DP) states that both are legitimate and necessary. It notes six qualities that should characterize the proclamation of the Gospel. First in line is confidence in the Holy Spirit, who "is present and active among the hearers of the Good News even before the Church's missionary activity comes into operation" (DP, no. 68). Then comes fidelity in the transmission of the teaching that is received from Christ and preserved in the Church. To faithfulness is joined humility, for the Revelation offered has been received as a free gift, and the messengers do not always live up to its demands. A fourth characteristic is respect for the presence and action of the Spirit of God in the hearts of those who listen. Because there may be "seeds of the Word" already present in the hearer, the process of proclamation is dialogical—the listener is not expected to be just a passive receiver. The final quality that should characterize the proclamation of the Gospel is that the message should be inculturated in the spiritual tradition and cultural context of the listeners to render it intelligible to them (DP, no. 70).

Taken all together, these five elements of Catholic evangelization—presence, service, prayer, dialogue, and proclamation—make up the "single but complex and articulated reality" of the Church's evangelizing mission and provide a picture of how evangelization happens (DM, no. 13). In looking at the overall list, one sees clearly that the evangelizing mission of the Church is not to be understood exclusively as an activity that has extending an invitation to membership in the Church as its goal.

Archbishop Michael Fitzgerald, president of the Vatican's Pontifical Council for Interreligious Dialogue, delivered a presentation on evangelization and interreligious dialogue to the Education for Parish Service Conference on October 25, 2003, in Washington, D.C. The archbishop made an important observation about the first four elements of evangelization: They are lived out for themselves and not for any ulterior purpose such as conversion to Christ.

> Presence and witness is already a way of practicing mission (and indeed this would be the way the Orthodox Churches see mission). Yet this presence and witness, to be authentic, has to be accompanied by prayer, both liturgical and non-liturgical. In the liturgy we proclaim Jesus Christ, yet we do not celebrate the liturgy in order to draw people to the Church. Of course the liturgy may be, and should be, attractive, and so may arouse interest among people who are not Christians who happen to be present, yet this is not its true purpose. The liturgy is celebrated to give glory to God. Similarly the service which the Church offers, in the fields of education, health, and care of all kinds, may also draw people to the Catholic fold, yet again this is not

its immediate aim. The Church has to engage in social action in order to express God's love for humankind, since the Church by nature is a sacrament of his divine love. So also dialogue should not be seen purely as a means to bring about conversions to Christianity; this would be too narrow a view, and would lead to dialogue being treated with suspicions by people of other religions. Dialogue can be taken as a way of reflecting God's love for all people, a love which respects their liberty.[11]

The presence of interreligious dialogue as one of the elements in the evangelizing mission of the Church warrants further development because it is the matter of most concern to the Church's partners in dialogue. The largely negative reaction to the declaration *On the Unicity and Salvific Universality of Jesus Christ and the Church* (hereafter *Dominus Iesus*), issued by the Congregation for the Doctrine of the Faith in 2000, centered around the declaration's statement that interreligious dialogue "is part of the Church's evangelizing mission."[12] What is the goal of such dialogue, and how has it come about that dialogue has been placed within the evangelizing mission of the Church?

The Goals of Interreligious Dialogue as an Element in the Church's Evangelizing Mission

Dominus Iesus was by no means the first time the link between interreligious dialogue and evangelization occurred in the Church's documents. It first occurred in *Dialogue and Mission* (1984), after which the pope asked the Pontifical Council for Interreligious Dialogue to give further development to this theme, but to do so in tandem with the Congregation for Evangelization of Peoples. The result of that work was *Dialogue and Proclamation* (1991). It is part of the working out during the post–Second Vatican Council years of a broad and comprehensive notion of evangelization in which dialogue represents a constitutive dimension. In this evolved understanding, dialogue is in itself a form of evangelization. How is this so?

As *Dialogue and Proclamation* says, "evangelization refers to the mission of the Church in its totality" (no. 8). Dialogue, an integral part of that mission, indicates "all positive and constructive interreligious relations with individuals and communities of other faiths which are directed at mutual understanding and enrichment. . . . in obedience to truth and respect for freedom" (no. 9). Announcement or proclamation is "the communication of the Gospel message, the mystery of salvation realized by God for all in Jesus Christ by the power of the Spirit. It is an invitation. . . to entry through baptism into the community of believers which is the Church (no. 10).

These distinctive definitions make clear that, while dialogue is already in itself evangelization, evangelization cannot be reduced to dialogue. The two are different in scope. They are intimately related but not interchangeable. Dialogue does not seek the conversion of others to Christianity, but rather, the convergence of both dialogue partners to a deeper shared conversion to God. By contrast, proclamation invites others to become disciples of Christ in the Christian community.

Commitment to dialogue, *Dialogue and Proclamation* declares, is something irreversible on the part of the Catholic Church. Christian participants in dialogue are expected to remain faithful to their identity as disciples of Jesus to whom they are called to give witness. But is the document also recognizes that, far from being an exercise that dilutes or compromises the essence of the Christian faith, engagement in interreligious dialogue provides an incentive for a Christian to become a better Christian. In fact, *Dialogue and Proclamation* makes this point clearly:

> Interreligious dialogue does not merely aim at mutual understanding and friendly relations. It reaches a much deeper level, that of the spirit, where exchange and sharing consist in a mutual witness to one's beliefs and a common exploration of one's respective religious convictions. In dialogue, Christians and others are invited to deepen their religious commitment. (no. 40)

Oftentimes people relate to interreligious dialogue at arm's length, fearful of falling into indifference and relativism. But the witness from those who do participate in it is quite different. The spiritual dimension is very real, and people actually grow in their faith and practice as a result of the interreligious encounter. One could even say that if this spiritual dimension is missing—if there is only academic exchange or friendly conversation—it is not an engaged interreligious dialogue. Let us call the first goal of interreligious dialogue, then, mutual enrichment.

Mutual Enrichment

In *Redemptoris Missio*, John Paul II gives further development to the question, "What are the goals of dialogue?" In interreligious dialogue, the Church seeks to discover the "seeds of the Word" that are found in the persons and in the religious traditions of humankind. The Church is stimulated "both to discover and acknowledge the signs of Christ's presence and of the working of the Spirit, as well as to examine more deeply her own identity and to bear witness to the fullness of Revelation which she has received for the good of all" (RM, no. 56).

Interreligious dialogue requires, in the words of *Dominus Iesus*, an attitude of "reciprocal enrichment, in obedience to the truth and with respect for freedom" (no. 2). The acknowledgements that Catholics might have something to learn from those who follow other religious traditions are not abundant, but they are exist. John Paul II notes, for example, in *The Redeemer of Man* (*Redemptor Hominis*) that the Church's "self-awareness" is formed by means of interreligious dialogue.[13] In *Redemptoris Missio*, interreligious dialogue is cited as "a method and means of mutual knowledge and enrichment" (no. 55) and as leading to "inner purification and conversion" of the Catholic partner to a deeper level of his or her own faith (no. 56).

Cardinal Walter Kaspar, president of the Pontifical Council that is responsible for dialogue with the Jews, has made it clear that dialogue is not a "one-way street," but rather, an "enrichment for us Christians" in which we are "not only the givers, but also the learners and receivers." That said, we must also recognize, that while mutual enrichment may be desirable as an ideal, other religious believers enter into dialogue with Catholics for a variety of reasons, and we should be neither naïve nor presumptuous about their motivations. Jews, for example, given their history of persecution, may be more drawn to dialogue by the opportunity to simply cultivate good relations than by the prospect of mutual enrichment.[14]

Dialogue and Mission also contributes to the theme of mutual enrichment in describing dialogue as a process in which Christians and people of other religious traditions "walk together towards the truth" (no. 13). Christians might instinctively respond, "Wait a minute! Didn't Jesus say 'I am the Way, the Truth, and the Life?' And if that's so, how can we who believe in Christ still be in search of the truth?" The 1991 document *Dialogue and Proclamation* responds,

> the fullness of truth received in Jesus Christ does not give individual Christians the guarantee that they have grasped that truth fully. In the last analysis truth is not a thing we possess, but a person by whom we must allow ourselves to be possessed. This is an unending process. While keeping their identity intact, Christians must be prepared to learn and to receive from and through others the positive values of their traditions." (no. 49)

61

The instance in which mutual enrichment is not only an attractive idea but a concrete necessity is that of interreligious marriage. In love's first bloom, a couple may share religious experience. Christmas at their parents' house may be joyous. The Jewish partner may participate in decorating the tree, attending midnight Mass, and celebrating the family meal. Chanukah may be celebrated with the Jewish family. On Passover, *Rosh Hashanah*, and *Yom Kippur,* the interfaith couple together may attend *Seder* dinner and High Holy Day services. Couples far from their families may do these rituals on their own.

But the adult fun of sharing traditions may disappear when such a couple has a child, if the interfaith sharing becomes competitive. And if both spouses are practicing their beliefs, it is difficult to avoid subtle manifestations of jockeying for a position of advantage in the raising of the child. The Christian would want Baptism and Confirmation. The Jew might want to attend a *Brit Milah* or *Brit Ha-Bat* and a *Bar/Bat Mitzvah*. Each ceremony connotes a commitment by parents to raise the child in the ways of the faith. In other cases, such as in Catholic-Muslim marriages, a determination of the question is built into the religion. According to Islamic law, the child of a Muslim father is a Muslim and has to be brought up as such. And since intermarriage between a Muslim woman and a non-Muslim man has always been forbidden in Islam, raising the children as Muslim is the lay of the land.

What previously a couple shared joyfully in their spiritual heritages can become a source of competition, irritation, personal loss, and disappointment. Therefore, it is of the utmost importance that candidates for interfaith marriages engage in open and honest dialogue about how they foresee their religious practice in the home and their raising of children. The pastoral wisdom to date is largely on the side of the children having a preferential relationship to one faith tradition and exposure to the other. The promise, either signed or given orally by the Catholic party to "do all in my power" to baptize and

---

The Holy Spirit, through the ecumenical movement, is calling churches and ecclesial communities into ever-deeper communion through dialogue and cooperation. We look forward with great eagerness to the day when all are members of one family.

—*Go and Make Disciples: A National Plan and Strategy for Catholic Evangelization in the United States* (Washington, DC: USCCB, 2002), no. 42

raise the children in the Catholic faith, is not a guarantee that this will in fact be the case. The eventual decision must be a joint decision in which both parents can cooperate. The children's religious upbringing is a joint responsibility of both partners. Hence, the promise, though a formative influence on the eventual decision, does not itself make that decision. The couple must put the unity of their marriage first, each one seeking to do the best he or she can in the concrete circumstances of their life together. A marital partnership is a life of compromises, and one partner may have to compromise more than the other does.

This leads us to a second goal in interreligious dialogue to help people live together in peace and harmony. When John Paul II addressed the world's religious leaders as they gathered to pray for peace at Assisi in 1986, he indicated that he was ready to acknowledge that Catholics have not always been faithful to this affirmation of faith, that we have not always been peacemakers. The Assisi gathering was therefore for the pope himself, and perhaps for all, an act of penance.[15]

In the New Testament, the metanoia to which Jesus calls us includes both repentance for sin and a new mind, a new way of looking at the world. Interreligious dialogue confronts Catholics and members of other traditions with a long list of requirements.

The first prerequisite for evangelizing others is to have entered into the process of conversion oneself. One of the most powerful images of this is that of John Paul II at the Western Wall in Jerusalem, praying for forgiveness for the sins of Catholics against Jews, and placing a piece of paper in the wall inscribed with words from the Vatican Lenten prayer service for forgiveness.

Some have felt that the apologies that the pope extended in every direction in the approach to the millennium were overdone. We have by no means finished with this process of purification of memory and examination of conscience. If we really take to heart evangelization in the context of interreligious dialogue, we have a great deal more work to do in reassessing passages in the New Testament relative to the Jews, the fathers of the Church, the medieval and baroque heritage, and the role of the Church in relation to other religions in more recent times.

In December 2001, an interfaith service took place in St. Paul's Episcopal Church next to "Ground Zero" in New York City. After each religious tradition offered prayers for peace in the church, everyone walked up onto the newly erected viewing platform that provided a direct sightline into the gaping hole where once the twin towers of the World Trade Center had stood. As we huddled together there in the cold under a starry sky, the Buddhists led a chant for all people to live together in peace and harmony. There could be no more dramatic image of the consequences of our failure to do so than the scene that was before us. Everyone present that night understood, more profoundly than ever, the importance of interreligious dialogue.

The occasion for such encounters also contributes to peace and harmony by promoting understanding among members of different traditions within the same religion. The Gethsemani II gathering of Catholic and Buddhist monastics at the Trappist monastery in Kentucky in 2002 provides an example. Whereas on the Christian side, we were all members of the same tradition of Christian faith (Catholic), on the Buddhist side, participants were from different Buddhist traditions. It was clear that our call to the Buddhists to spend four days in interreligious dialogue provided them with a rare and privileged opportunity to pursue harmony, respect, and understanding among themselves. The opportunity for such internal communication bears its own good fruits, and it is often an overlooked but significant contribution to people living together in harmony and peace.

This second goal of interreligious dialogue gives way to a third: collaboration in the service of humankind. This one seems so evident as to need little development. Most states and large cities now have interreligious councils with programs relating to hunger, the environment, the homeless, religious liberty, the elderly, the handicapped, and refugees.

To see how all this relates to the Reign of God, one only needs to look at Jesus' words in Matthew 25:31-40 about the criteria that will be used when the Son of Man comes in his glory and sits on his throne with all the nations gathered before him. After being directed to his right like sheep separated from goats, the righteous will ask him,

> Lord, when did we see you hungry and feed you, or thirsty and give you drink? When did we see you a stranger and welcome you, or naked and clothe you? When did we see you ill or in prison, and visit you? (Mt 25: 37-39)

And he will answer them: "Amen, I say to you, whatever you did for one of these least brothers of mine, you did for me" (Mt 25: 40).

This New Testament passage begs a further question: What is the role of Christ, the Holy Spirit, and the Church in the salvation of those who end up at the right hand of the Son of Man? Since the Second Vatican Council, the theology of religious pluralism has shifted the discussion about adherents of other religions from whether they can be saved to how they are saved. To respond to this question, we must look at some of the theological foundations for interreligious dialogue as a constituent element in the Church's overall evangelizing mission.

Dialogue and Proclamation invokes a threefold theological foundation for interreligious dialogue—the common origin and the single destiny of the human race in God, universal salvation in Jesus Christ, the active presence of the Holy Spirit—and infers a fourth: the universality of the Reign of God.

Common Origin and Destiny of Humankind

The Constitution on the Church in the Modern World (*Gaudium et Spes*) teaches that "since Christ died for all men, and since the ultimate vocation of man is in fact one, and divine, we ought to believe that the Holy Spirit in a manner known only to God offers to every man the possibility of being associated with this paschal mystery."[16] In an important speech to members of the Roman Curia on December 22, 1986, John Paul II took the theological foundation of dialogue presented by the Council—the unity of origin and of destiny of the human race through creation and redemption—as a "mystery of unity" that unites all human beings, whatever the differences in their circumstances might be: "The differences are a less important element than the unity which, by contrast, is radical, basic, and decisive" (no. 3). This universal unity, the pope said, "based on the event of creation and redemption, cannot but leave a trace in the reality lived by human beings, even those belonging to different religions" (no. 7).[17]

Universal Salvation in Jesus Christ

"Go out to the highways and hedgerows and make people come in that my home may be filled" (Lk:14:23). The great banquet in Luke embodies Jesus' vision of God's Reign. It is a global vision. The participation of all in the banquet symbolizes the participation of all in God's salvation. The full house of the banquet symbolizes the universality of belonging to the Reign of God. It becomes a banquet for all the people, even the outcasts and the foreigners. As *Dialogue and Proclamation* points out, the miracles that Jesus worked for foreigners like the Canaanite woman (Mt 15:21) and the Roman centurion (Mt 8:10) have the same meaning that he gives to all his other miracles (DP, no. 21). These miracles mean that the Reign of God is already present and at work among the Gentiles—the nations—as well. Jesus' message is that, in his own person, the Reign of God is breaking through to the world—and not just to his followers.

The Active Presence of the Holy Spirit

A post-conciliar motif is that the Spirit of God is universally present and operative in the religious life of others (non-Catholics) and in the religious traditions to which they belong. This emphasis does not appear in the writings of Paul VI, but it is a recurring theme in the teaching of his successor, John Paul II. The presence and universal action of the Spirit of God among the others and in their religious traditions represents John Paul II's most important contribution to the theological foundation of interreligious dialogue.[18]

In his encyclical *On the Holy Spirit in the Life of the Church and the World* (*Dominum et Vivificantem*) (DV), John Paul II writes that the action of the Spirit "exercised, in every place and at every time, indeed in every individual."[19] In *Redemptoris Missio*, he goes further, saying that "The Spirit's presence and activity affect not only the individuals but also society and history, peoples, cultures and religions" (no. 28). In *Redemptor Hominis*, he sees even the "firm belief" of the followers of other religions as "an effect of the Spirit of truth operating outside the visible confines of the Mystical Body" (no. 6). "We may think," he says, "that any authentic prayer is aroused by the Holy Spirit, who is mysteriously present in the heart of every human being" (RM no. 29).

These perspectives of faith mean that wherever we go, the Spirit has gone ahead of us. We are not, then, going to people of other religions as though we have all truth, and as though they have only illusion and falsehood. Rather we go with a sharp eye and ear for everything that is good, noble, inspiring, and beautiful in their rites and traditions. When we encounter methods of prayer, ethical rules, and spiritual teachings that encourage transcendence of our own selfish inclinations in seeking the good of others, our response is one of appreciation and respect. Thus does the interfaith encounter become a journey of discovery and an occasion of mutual enrichment.

The Universality of the Reign of God

Redemptoris Missio is the first document of the Roman Magisterium to keep united but to distinguish clearly between the Church and the Kingdom of God in their pilgrimage through history. The Reign of God is not coterminous with the Church. Extending the Reign of God is not simply increasing the membership in the Church. God's Reign is advancing in ways unknown to us, through the Church, certainly, but also through other ways, among other people. By responding in the sincere practice of their religious traditions to God's call addressed to them, followers of other religious paths truly become—albeit without being formally conscious of it—active members of the Reign. Their religious traditions contribute in a mysterious manner to the construction of the Reign of God in the world.

As we have examined the various elements in the Church's evangelizing mission, such as the struggle for justice and peace or mutual understanding and respect through dialogue, we have noted how each contributes to the realization of the Reign of God in a particular time and place. Christians and members of other religions are walking together, joint members of the Reign of God in history, toward the fullness of that new humanity willed by God for the end of time, of which they are called to be co-creators under God.

Dialogue and Proclamation: Partner Expressions of Evangelization

"All Christians are called to be personally involved in these two ways of carrying out the one mission of the church, namely, proclamation and dialogue" (DP, no 82). These two elements exist in a dialectical relationship in the dynamic process of the Church's evangelizing mission. There is an inescapable tension between them—the tension between the "already" and the "not yet," Insofar as the Church remains on her pilgrimage together with the non-Christians toward the fullness of the Reign of God, she engages with them in dialogue. Insofar as she is the sacrament of the reality of the Reign of God already present and operative in history, she proclaims to them Jesus Christ in whom the Reign has been established.[20]

The Roman Catholic Church today is hard at work in both developing its understanding of evangelization and in developing a Christian theology of religious pluralism. Both are works in progress. This is the context for the ambiguities and fluctuations in emphasis of various Vatican documents. It is a complex task, and the complexity requires us to be mindful of the details and the nuances in reading, on the one hand, the Council's decree On the Mission Activity of the Church (Ad Gentes) and Paul VI's apostolic exhortation On Evangelization in the Modern World, and on the other hand, the Pontifical Council for Interreligious Dialogue's documents Dialogue and Mission and Dialogue and Proclamation.[21]

Take, for example, a sentence in *Dialogue and Proclamation* that exemplifies the necessity of attention to nuances, in which dialogue "does not constitute the whole mission of the Church, that it cannot simply replace proclamation, but remains oriented towards proclamation in so far as the dynamic process of the Church's evangelizing mission reaches in it its climax and its fullness (no. 82). This is true enough.

At the same time, interreligious dialogue is a legitimate form of evangelization even though in many dialogues no proclamation or catechesis takes place. Dialogue is oriented towards proclamation in one strict sense: in proclamation the dynamic process of evangelization reaches its climax. This does not mean that we enter interreligious dialogue in order to announce and catechize. The "orientation" of dialogue toward proclamation corresponds to the "orientation" of adherents of other religious traditions toward the Church.[22] They are "oriented" to it because to it is entrusted "the fullness of the benefits and the means of salvation" (RM, no. 18).

Dialogue, in other words, is included in the Church's evangelizing mission because it is part of the real work of the Church. As Catholics engage in dialogue with members of other living faiths, it is important that there be no ambiguity about their intentions in the minds of their partners. "Dialogue," as Paul VI said, "cannot be a tactical snare."[23] It is a form of sharing, of giving and receiving. It is not a one-way process. It must really be a dialogue, not a monologue.

Such an inbuilt tension between the Church's outreach to its neighbors in dialogue and its missionary effort is inescapable. Given the Church's complex relationships with other communities in a religiously diverse world, and given its own internal dialogue on these questions, it would be both unrealistic and surprising to expect anything else than the delicate exercise of holding the two points of a fulcrum in tense balance.[24]

In its *Theses on Interreligious Dialogue*, the Theological Advisory Commission of the Federation of Asian Bishops recognized that the Church does not monopolize God's action in the world. While it is aware of a special mission of God upon earth, the Church has to be attentive to God's action in the world, as manifested also in other religions. This twofold awareness constitutes the two poles of the Church's evangelizing action—dialogue and proclamation—in relation to other religions.[25]

Proclamation is the expression of the Church's awareness of being in mission. Dialogue is the expression of its awareness of God's presence and action outside its boundaries. Proclamation is the affirmation of and witness to God's action in oneself and in the Church. Dialogue is the openness and attention to the mystery of God's action in the other believer. We cannot speak of one without the other. *Dialogue and Proclamation* states:

> Interreligious dialogue and proclamation, though not on the same level, are both authentic elements of the Church's evangelizing mission. Both are legitimate and necessary. They are intimately related, but not interchangeable. . . . The two activities remain distinct, but one and the same local Church, one and the same person, can be diversely engaged in both. (no. 77)

To say such things about proclamation would surprise no one familiar with the way the Church has traditionally talked about its mission; of course announcing the Good News is "necessary," "essential," and never to be interchanged with anything else. But can we say the same about dialogue? This is an astonishingly new emphasis. To make sure we get the message, the Vatican document presses the point: proclamation is "only one aspect of evangelization" that needs to be balanced with other aspects and can never be interchanged with them (DP, no. 8). When one looks not only at what the Vatican documents *Dialogue and Mission* and *Dialogue and Proclamation* have to say about the essential place that dialogue plays in the mission of the Church but also at the way they describe such dialogue, one is led to the conclusion that this new emphasis constitutes an adjustment—if not a paradigm shift—in how the Catholic Magisterium understands mission.[26]

The juxtaposition of proclamation and dialogue as partner expressions of evangelization calls us to recognize that we have something to gain from both ecumenical and interreligious dialogue. Our own faith will be enriched. We will be able to discover at greater depth, through the experience and testimony of others, certain aspects and dimensions of the divine mystery. We will gain a clarification and a purification of our faith as the encounter with the other raises questions and forces us to revise gratuitous assumptions. We will uproot deep-seated prejudices and overturn certain narrow conceptions and outlooks.

Because of these fruits, we must say that the encounter and the exchange have value in themselves. They are an end in themselves. While from the outset, they presuppose openness to the other and to God, they also effect a deeper openness to God in each through the other. If the goal of proclamation is conversion to Christ in the Church, the goal of dialogue is deeper conversion of all toward God. As Fr. Jacques Dupuis, SJ, summarizes it:

Thus dialogue does not serve as a means to a further end. Neither on one side nor on the other does it tend to the "conversion" of one's partners to one's own religious tradition. Rather it tends toward a deeper conversion of each to God. The same God speaks in the heart of both partners; the same Spirit is at work in both. It is the same God who calls and challenges the partners through one another, by means of their mutual witness. Thus they become, as it were, for each other and reciprocally, a sign leading to God. The proper end of the interreligious dialogue is ultimately the common conversion of Christians and the members of other religious traditions to the same God—the God of Jesus Christ—who calls them together with one another, challenging them through each other. This reciprocal call, a sign of God's call, is surely mutual evangelization. It builds up, between members of various religious traditions, the universal communion which marks the advent of the Reign of God.[27]

Fr. Thomas Ryan, CSP

Fr. Thomas Ryan, CSP, directs the Paulist North American Office for Ecumenical and Interfaith Relations in New York City. He previously served for fourteen years as director of the Canadian Center for Ecumenism and founded an ecumenical center for spirituality called Unitas in Montreal, Canada. He has authored seven books, preaches for ecumenical parish missions, and leads ecumenical retreats in the United States, Canada, and Europe.

NOTES

1 Paul VI, *On Evangelization in the Modern World* (*Evangelii Nuntiandi*) (Washington, DC: Libreria Editrice Vaticana–USCCB, 1999), no. 14. Subsequent citations are given in the text.

2 John Paul II, *On the Permanent Validity of the Church's Missionary Mandate* (*Redemptoris Missio*) (Washington, DC: Libreria Editrice Vaticana–USCCB, 1998), nos. 33-34. Subsequent citations are given in the text.

3 United States Conference of Catholic Bishops, *Go and Make Disciples: A National Plan and Strategy for Catholic Evangelization in the United States*. Tenth Anniversary English and Spanish Edition. (Washington, DC: USCCB, 2002), nos. 4-5. Subsequent citations are given in the text.

4 Paul VI, *On the Church* (*Ecclesiam Suam*) (Vatican City: Libreria Editrice Vaticana, August 6, 1964), nos. 65-69.

5 Cf. Vatican Secretariat for Non-Christians, *The Attitude of the Church toward the Followers of Other Religions: Reflections and Orientations on Dialogue and Mission* (Vatican City: Pentecost, 1984) and Pontifical Council for Interreligious Dialogue, *Dialogue and Proclamation: Reflection and Orientations on Interreligious Dialogue and the Proclamation of the Gospel of Jesus Christ* (Vatican City: Libreria Editrice Vaticana, May 19, 1991). Subsequent citations are given in the text.

6 John Paul II, "To the Plenary Sessions of the Secretariat for Non-Christians" (Vatican City: Libreria Editrice Vaticana, March 3, 1984), no. 270, *Interreligious Dialogue: The Official Teachings of the Catholic Church 1963-1995*, Francesco Gioia, ed. (Boston: Pauline Books and Media, 1997), no. 421.

7 John Paul II, "To the Plenary Sessions," no. 270.

8   Vatican Secretariat for Non-Christians, *The Attitude of the Church toward the Followers of Other Religions: Reflections and Orientations on Dialogue and Mission* (Vatican City: Libreria Editrice Vaticana, Pentecost, 1984) in *Interreligious Dialogue: The Official Teachings of the Catholic Church 1963-1995*, Francesco Gioia, ed. (Boston: Pauline Books and Media, 1997), no. 820.

9   As recounted in Ronald Roberson, CSP, *The Eastern Churches*, 6th ed. (Vatican City: Edizioni Orientalia Christiania, 1999), no. 60.

10 Edith Stein, *Life in a Jewish Family: Her Unfinished Autobiographical Account*, ed. L. Gelber and Romaeus Leuven, trans. Josephine Koeppel (Washington, DC: ICS Publications, 1986).

11 Archbishop Michael Fitzgerald, "Evangelization and Interreligious Dialogue," *Origins* 33:23 (November 13, 2003): 403.

12 Congregation for the Doctrine of the Faith, *On the Unicity and Salvific Universality of Jesus Christ and the Church* (*Dominus Iesus*) (Vatican City: Libreria Editrice Vaticana, June 16, 2000), no. 2.

13 John Paul II, *The Redeemer of Man* (*Redemptor Hominis*) (Vatican City: Libreria Editrice Vaticana, March 4, 1979).

14 James Fredericks, "The Catholic Church and Other Religious Paths: Rejecting Nothing That Is True and Holy," in *Theological Studies* 64 (Marquette: 2003): 251-252.

15 Cf. John Paul II, Address to the Representatives of the Christian Churches and Ecclesial Communities Gathered in Assisi for the World Day of Prayer (October 27, 1986).

16 Second Vatican Council, *Constitution on the Church in the Modern World* (*Gaudium et Spes*) (Washington, DC: Libreria Editrice Vaticana–USCCB, 1996), no. 22.

17 Pontifical Commission, "Justitia et Paix," in *Assise: Journée Mondiale de Prière pour la Paix* (October 26, 1986): 147-155.

18 Fr. Jacques Dupuis, SJ, *Christianity and the Religions: From Confrontation to Dialogue*, trans. Phillip Berryman (Maryknoll, NY: Orbis Books, 2002), 223.

19 John Paul II, *On the Holy Spirit in the Life of the Church and the World (Dominum et Vivificantem)* (Vatican City: Libreria Editrice Vaticana, May 18, 1986), no. 53.

20 Dupuis, 225-226.

21 Second Vatican Council, *On the Mission Activity of the Church (Ad Gentes Divinitus)* (Vatican City: Libreria Editrice Vaticana, December 7, 1965).

22 Paul VI, *Dogmatic Constitution on the Church (Lumen Gentium)* (Vatican City: Libreria Editrice Vaticana, November 21, 1964), no. 16.

23 "To the Catholic Associations of the Italian Workers," *Interreligious Dialogue: The Official Teachings of the Catholic Church 1963-1995*, Francesco Gioia, ed. (Boston: Pauline Books and Media, 1997), no. 217.

24 Fredericks, 251.

25 "Documents of the Church in Asia: Theses on Interreligious Dialogue" in *Dialogue: Resource Manual for Catholics in Asia* (Bangkok: Federation of Asian Bishops, 2001), 85-95.

26 Paul Knitter, "Mission as Dialogue," in *Dialogue: Resource Manual for Catholics in Asia* (Bangkok: Federation of Asian Bishops, 2001), 82-83.

27 Dupuis, 225-226.

Prayer Service

The Very Rev. Keith A. Marsh

There is a literary device, quite popular in movies of the 1930s and 1940s, used in films we might associate with actors like Basil Rathbone and Myrna Loy—movies now shown on late-night television that are standard fare for insomniacs. This somewhat clichéd cinematic formula involves a group of people who have come together, or more accurately, who have been thrown together, through some strange set of circumstances. The formula requires that they must be gathered around a roaring fire, relaxing after dinner in some huge, isolated, English manor house. And they are always overdressed: the men in tuxedoes, brandy snifters and cigars in hand, striking overly masculine poses; the women in long gowns, sitting about the room, striking overly feminine poses. There is always one rather saucy, independent dame to whom the men are attracted and by whom the other women are threatened. This cinematic formula requires that a storm be raging outside: lightning flashing occasionally through long casement windows, loud cracks of thunder periodically sending the women—all except the self-assured one—shrieking into the arms of the men, who never appear to have heard the noise, much less to have been scared by it.

Readings:
Acts 2:1-11
Jn 1:1-14

In this scene, the door suddenly blows open! A stranger appears! Drenched, disheveled, barely alive from having been caught in the storm, he is a stark contrast to the others into whose presence he now comes. Alarmed, the women again run to the men's arms; even the saucy dame seems a bit shaken. Straining against the strong wind and driving rain, someone struggles to close the door. The stranger is somewhat reluctantly brought near the fire and made comfortable, often because someone reminds the group that "it is, after all, the only Christian thing to do."

Then, after a long, slow sip of brandy, the stranger begins to tell a story, slowly weaving a tale. And this is not just any story, but one that fully engages the others, seductively drawing them in as if they are spellbound. Being the perceptive audience that we are—and because we understand how this literary formula works—we know that this stranger's tale will, in some mysterious, inexplicable way, dramatically affect and forever change the lives of all those who hear it.

The storyteller finishes his tale. Strangely, the dark night of the storm always ends at just the same time, and the first light of a bright new dawn begins to flood the room. The storyteller, his role now completed, quickly and mysteriously departs. The other characters, those who first gathered together, now enter into the second half of the formula—figuring out why they were told this tale and slowly learning how the stranger's story now comes to life, becoming their life story. The storyteller leaves, and the others are left asking the question, "What does this mean?"

Some things can only be told as story, as narrative, as tale. Like the characters in the movie, someone offers us a story. A family member, a friend, a neighbor, or a co-worker offers us a tale. We listen; we receive it, and then we are left to ask, "What does this mean? Why was I told this? What am I supposed to do with this?"

Often there may be no immediate or obvious answers to these questions. Sometime the story is given to us for one purpose—that we receive it . . . and wait: wait for the story to become true; wait for the story to make sense in our own experience; wait for the reality of the story to be made known in our lives.

The narrative of the first Pentecost is such a tale. Like our mysterious stranger, the Spirit and its story come quickly. And like those overdressed men and women in our film, the assembled crowd, those to whom the Gospel story had suddenly been given in their native languages, ask, "What does this mean?"

Even the author of the Book of Acts, recounting this event that gives birth to the Church, is at a loss to describe and explain the phenomenon. But he is sure of one thing: that something of immense power and significance has taken place. But how it happened—what exactly it is that happened—well, he searches for words and images to tell the tale:

Suddenly there came from the sky a noise like a strong driving wind" (Acts 2:2).

A wind! That's it! A wind! But it is something more, something only "like" a wind.

"There appeared to them tongues as of fire, which parted and came to rest on each one of them" (Acts 2:3).

Fire! Yes! That's it! But it is something more—not just fire, but something "as of fire."

Unlike our Sunday School illustrations, these are not easy, comfortable images. They describe a Spirit who comes with the suddenness of a tornado, the terror of a firestorm. As described in Scripture, the arrival of the Holy Spirit is not an easy comfortable image, but one that is disturbing, even terrifying. And rightfully so, for the Spirit comes with ferocity and force.

If we read a few verses further into the story, even Peter, "the rock," the practical, seemingly unflappable disciple, stands shaken to the core by the Pentecost experience. And when he addresses the crowd, his thoughts and words are a jumble of poetry and psalm and somewhat incoherent explanation.

There are no neat explanations here, no slick analysis of what has occurred. Why? Because there cannot be! It is impossible to follow the shattering experience of Pentecost, the receiving of the Holy Spirit, the sudden indwelling of God, with some tidy piece of systematic theology. And so the story is told—just told! it is told as best it can be, told for us to hear, told for us to receive, told for us to take with us—offered, that we may receive it and wait. We must wait for it to become true in our own experience, wait for it to make sense, wait for it to change us. The Spirit comes with ferocity and force, and like those first Christian disciples, we are left asking, "What does this mean?"

Is there meaning for us? Can there be meaning for us as twenty-first-century people in an event that happened in a room halfway around the world, in another culture, almost two thousand years ago? The story-teller of Acts, and Christians down through the ages, have understood the Pentecost event as an indicator: whatever the birth, life, death, and Resurrection of Jesus Christ means, it is above all a reality of universal significance, a story with meaning for all humanity, for all creation, for all time. The Good News of the Gospel is not merely of significance for a particular culture or a unique race or nation, but it is also significant for everyone who will gather to hear and receive the story.

As the Church gathers to celebrate this event each year, the opening collect for the Feast of Pentecost, reads as follows: "Almighty God, on this day you opened the way of eternal life to every race and nation by the promised gift of your Holy Spirit. Shed abroad this gift throughout the world by the preaching of the Gospel, that it may reach the ends of the earth."[1]

In prayer, we acknowledge and are reminded that in some inexplicable way, Jesus has "opened a way"—a way for a new quality of life, a way to regain a lost dimension of our intended, true, whole humanity. This universal, eternal, life-giving aspect of the story continues to unfold. It remains as true, yet unexplainable, today in this room, as it was inexplicably true two thousand years ago in a room in Jerusalem. This truth permeates the Gospel story until the end of time, for men and women of all races and all nations.

The Holy Spirit comes suddenly, forcefully, first destroying, then creating. In Baptism, the living God takes us by force, entering our humanity and forever changing us. We are right to be fearful, even terrified, for we are surrendering ourselves to be destroyed, in the hope of being newly created.

This opening of a way for our new creation—a way to redeem our intended human fullness, a way to eternal life through Jesus Christ— was the truth proclaimed and shed abroad by the early disciples. Indeed, the early Church was actually called "The Way" before she was labeled "Christian." And throughout the centuries, this claim, this truth, this miraculous, glorious, inexplicable "meaning" of the story remained: a way to eternal life in our Creator was now open through the death and Resurrection of Jesus Christ.

Unfortunately, we need only read the accounts of the Crusades, the brutal missionary tactics used throughout the Americas, and the pogroms of Eastern Europe to see the abusing of this truth, the forcing of "the only way," and the pressing of this gift upon others. With missionary zeal, we have tried to emulate the work of the Holy Spirit. And too often, in the wake of the destruction of foreign cultures and peoples, we attempted to recreate our own image, mistaking it for the image of God.

But while we can and must stop arrogantly superimposing our faith on the other great religious traditions and cultures, we cannot and must not stop offering knowledge and access to "The Way" we have found— or more correctly, "The Way" that has found us. Inviting others to join in our faith journey is the ultimate living out of our experience of God's truth, the ultimate gift of grace to those who choose to gather and hear and receive the story we have to tell. To share our story with others is to incarnate the Gospel story in our place, in our own time.

We have been offered a wondrous gift! We have received a marvelous gift, a gift beyond price! And like most gifts of value, it brings a responsibility. "As the Father has sent me, so I send you" (Jn 20:21). This charge to evangelism and ministry shapes the lives of all who hear it in ways we never dreamed of, transforming lives and communities and nations in ways the world never dreamed of.

And once heard, the charge becomes impossible to ignore: "As the Father has sent me, so I send you." We have heard and received the story. We have heard and received the charge. But what does that mean? What are we supposed to do with it?

Simply put, the Gospel recounts the intersection of the human and the divine in the person of Jesus Christ. Simply put, in the waters of Baptism, we too become that place of intersection and intervention. We are, each one of us, a Gospel incarnate. And each of us must speak and live out our own experience of the Gospel story, recount our version of the tale, share our experience of the Holy Spirit, give our knowledge and experience of the way that has become our way, and offer our limited but valuable and insightful answers to the question, What does this mean?

Jesus commands, "As the Father has sent me, so I send you." But where do we gain the courage to speak? Where do we get the strength to risk offering ourselves, our experience, our knowledge, and our beliefs of the truth and the way? Where do we gain the fortitude and resolve to make ourselves vulnerable and open ourselves to the possibility of being misunderstood or even ridiculed? How do we offer and share this great gift that we have received?

Before Jesus' death, he reassured his followers that they would not be abandoned. The Advocate, the Spirit of God's truth, this forceful Spirit, would come to guide and inspire them. In the midst of questioning and fear, the Spirit would create them anew. And to these newly created children of God, the Spirit brings an abiding sense of peace, a peace that only our Creator—and our re-Creator!—can give.

Theological understanding, our personal knowledge of the living God, springs forth from this experience of peace in Jesus Christ—the inner security and release from fear that comes through prayer and a trusting relationship in God. Those first disciples who gathered in that upper room, and those of us gathered here this evening, are able to go forth and tell the story—the Gospel story—which is now made our story and shines forth in our lives We are able to share our story with confidence, made secure in the peace of God as revealed and made known to us in the sacramental life of the Church.

Neither we nor those first disciples were sent out alone, any more than Jesus was sent forth alone. The Holy Spirit was with the Son in his earthly ministry, empowering him to do the work of the Father. That same work, now entrusted to us the Church to accomplish through our earthly ministries, requires that same Spirit. "Receive the Holy Spirit!" is as potent a proclamation and as powerful a gift for us today as it was on that first Pentecost. The same Spirit that drove Jesus into the wilderness following his Baptism drove those first disciples into the streets to proclaim the Gospel in many tongues.

That same Spirit continues to drive the Church, and it continues to drive each of us out into the world. In the Spirit, we are emboldened with the security of God's peace and love for us. We are made confident to offer ourselves in the service of that divine, life-giving love offered for each of us.

What does this mean, this powerful, miraculous, inexplicable story of Pentecost? It is passed along to us, and we have received it. We wait for it to become real in our lives. We nourish it with our faithfulness. This Gospel story becomes our own story through Baptism and belief.

We ask, "What does this mean?" Then, somehow—whether in a flash of revelation, or gradually—we come to know that the work of living a life of faith in Christ is important, but that sharing that life, revealing the Gospel of the living God, and inviting others into the journey, becomes our most faithful life's work.

Brothers and sisters in Christ:

Receive and lay claim to the Holy Spirit!

Know the peace of God that passes all understanding!

Make Christ known in and through your life!

For that is our life's work—the work of faithful and faith-filled discipleship!

Amen.

The Very Rev. Keith A. Marsh

Fr. Marsh graduated from Indiana University in 1974 with a BS in marketing/advertising. In 1991, he received an M Div degree from the Virginia Theological Seminary. He is currently enrolled in a master of theology/liturgy degree program at the University of Notre Dame in Indiana. He has served as a member and chair of many diocesan and community-wide commissions and ministries. He served as associate rector of St. Matthew's Church in Louisville, Kentucky, from 1991 to 1995, and he has been the dean of Christ Church Cathedral in Louisville since 1996.

NOTE

1   Church of England, *The Book of Common Prayer*, 1st. American ed. (New York: Henry Holt, 1992), 227.